WAR INTERLUDE

1916 – 1919

Harold Hesler

Edited by William Hesler

iUniverse, Inc.
Bloomington

War Interlude 1916 – 1919

iUniverse books may be ordered through booksellers or by contacting:

iUniverse
1663 Liberty Drive
Bloomington, IN 47403
www.iuniverse.com
1-800-Authors (1-800-288-4677)

Because of the dynamic nature of the Internet, any web addresses or links contained in this book may have changed since publication and may no longer be valid. The views expressed in this work are solely those of the author and do not necessarily reflect the views of the publisher, and the publisher hereby disclaims any responsibility for them.

Any people depicted in stock imagery provided by Thinkstock are models, and such images are being used for illustrative purposes only.

Certain stock imagery © Thinkstock.

ISBN: 978-1-4620-0352-5 (sc)
ISBN: 978-1-4620-0354-9 (ebook)
ISBN: 978-1-4620-0353-2 (dj)

Printed in the United States of America

iUniverse rev. date: 3/31/2011

Note on the cover illustration

Included with Harold Hesler's manuscript of *War Interlude* is a clipping from the *New York Times Magazine* of November 10, 1940. It was the illustration for an article by the American journalist and WWI vet Samuel Williamson, with the title *"Was it worth it?"*. It is an etching by the war artist Kerr Eby, with the caption *"Rough going"*. Under the drawing appear the words of the article's author:

> *"But in all the filth and stupidities of that experience I saw courage, fortitude, sacrifice"*[1]

Under the clipping, Harold Hesler has written simply:

> "The words might almost be mine".

---

1 The full quote reads: "But in all the filth and stupidities of that experience I saw courage, fortitude, sacrifice, self-abnegation, generosity yes, and tenderness, compassion and idealism of a quality and an amount that I have not seen since".

311,972 DRIVER HAROLD HESLER,
NO. 3 SECTION, 3ᴿᴰ DIVISIONAL AMMUNITION COLUMN

"I also had my photograph taken in Winnipeg which shows me as I felt."

EDITOR'S NOTE

Harold Hesler completed work on his *War Interlude* in the Spring of 1962—more than four decades after he returned to Canada from the First World War. In 2010, I published *Muleskinner: The European War of a Niagara Artilleryman*. In *Muleskinner*, I tried to put my father's experiences in context. I wanted to give the reader an understanding of Canada's involvement in the conflict, and a sense of what lay behind the generally light-hearted account which he gives in *War Interlude*.

The text which follows is exactly as my father wrote it, except for the insertion of accents in French place names, and the section headings. I have also added the illustrations, as well as the extracts from the official Divisional Ammunition Column war diaries.

As explained in *Muleskinner*, the title of Harold Hesler's reminiscences reflects the fact that the three and a half years he spent in the Canadian Artillery were the only moments in his working life when he was not with the Royal Bank of Canada. He retired from the Bank in 1951, and died just before his eighty-ninth birthday in 1982.

W.H. 24 February 2011

FOREWORD

This is an account of my experiences during World War I. It is based principally on diary notes which I jotted down as I moved about in France and Belgium and during periods of leave in Paris, England, Scotland and Ireland. Over the years I had attempted at many times to expand these into a narrative; this was not accomplished until April 1962.

H. G. Hesler
Westmount, April 10th, 1962.

CHAPTER ONE

1916

Winnipeg

When war was declared in August 1914 I was approaching my twenty-first birthday and was Accountant at the Chapleau branch of The Royal Bank of Canada, a rather isolated point in northern Ontario, and until I left there in May 1915 I gave only casual consideration to enlisting for service. The movement of troop trains on their way to Valcartier through this divisional point on the main line of the Canadian Pacific Railway did nudge my conscience to a degree when at times I thought that I ought to join my lot with these men who were travelling east with so much enthusiasm, but my life up to this time had been so distant from anything bearing on the military that it was not difficult to bury these feelings throughout the severe northern winter. In May 1915 I was transferred to Sault Sainte Marie where the spirit of the times was more evident but I was barely settled there when, in July, I was moved to Winnipeg. This bustling city was alive with troops of one sort or another and the atmosphere made it increasingly apparent to me that my own opinion of my incapacity for military duty was not a valid reason for not attempting to do what was called "one's bit". John Zoller, who had been with me for some time in the bank at Chapleau, was transferred to Winnipeg in the fall and moved into the apartment which I had been sharing with my brother Norman, who left for the east about this time. John and I talked the matter over every night, sometimes after only a light snack as our finances were very slim, and finally in December we decided to take the plunge and to take it in earnest. That is we made up our minds to go in for something out of the ordinary, something super-dangerous and thereby even the balance which in our conscience we felt was against us through our tardiness. After much consideration and investigation we found that a section of the Third Divisional Ammunition Column would be recruited in Winnipeg at the turn of the year and it was represented to us as one of the most spectacular arms of the service since the cavalry had been dismounted. In fact, the Air Force seemed dull in comparison when we were told of all the dashing about that an Ammunition Column did in delivering small arms ammunition to the infantry and shells to the artillery. We did not know that by the time we would arrive at the Front the artillery establishment would be reorganized to change all of this. We knew a little about horses from our boyhood days but neither of us had done much riding. Nothing daunted, we gave the required one month's notice to the bank and on January 20, 1916 we signed on with No. 3 Section, 3rd Divisional Ammunition Column. John was given number 311,971 and I received 311,972.

ANOTHER BATTERY TO BE MOBILIZED

Recruiting for Ammunition Column Starts Soon — Many Provisional Appointments.

Military orders yesterday announce mobilization of a new overseas battery C.F.A., the 44th under the command of C. E. Gregory. No. 3 section divisional ammunition column will also be mobilized, recruiting commencing on Jan. 1. Quarters have been obtained in the Alloway building, McDermot avenue east. Capt. T. W. Stevens, of the 37th overseas battery, will be in charge of the section.

EXTRACT FROM THE MANITOBA FREE PRESS
DECEMBER 31, 1915

Our barracks consisted of one floor of an old building on McDermot Avenue just off Main Street and was furnished with a mass of double-decker bunks, with no space to walk, stand or sit except in the narrow aisles between the rows of bunks or on our bunks. On the upper floor was another military outfit recently down from Prince Albert where they had been recruited as the nucleus of an infantry battalion, but falling far short of the establishment were now being transformed into a battery of artillery. What a rough, tough and noisy crowd they were. We had no cooking facilities in our building so three times a day we marched a few cold blocks to a large hall that served as a community kitchen for several units. We had no horses so we marched out to the Exhibition Grounds several times a week and were there introduced to the horses of the 43rd Battery which was to form a part of the Third Divisional Artillery—fortunately there was lots of snow to fall into and not enough horses for everyone to be mounted on every visit. We had no place for foot drill except in the streets or in school yards, but we did occasionally attend lectures and light exercise drills in the old Bank of Hamilton Building on Main Street which had been condemned and otherwise vacated and the floor wavered under every footstep. How Lieut. Miles would swear at us and Sergeant Preston would berate us when we were slow at grasping the elements of mounted drill on foot or for falling off a horse! I developed a charley-horse which the massages of the medical officer could not erase and he finally told me he would have to recommend my discharge. I still thought that I was going to be a modern Crusader so I hid my pain and eventually worked it out of my system. Hardening but not heartening. Fortunately one thing was true—we were not going to spend a long time in training in Canada.

Our full number was recruited by the end of February. We had group photographs taken, one of the whole section and others of the half-sections. There were a few additions and discharges before we went overseas but most of the men who made the journey are in the photographs. There were also some switches of men from one half-section to the other. My only copies of these photographs were destroyed in a cyclone in Havana in 1926 and I recovered one of our half-section from brother Norman which is part of this record[2]. By that time I could not remember all of the names of the men in my half-section but I had

2   Ed.: the half-section photo has been reproduced in the Appendices, with three close-ups for better identification of those present.

been able to save a list of the men on the strength in February 1916 compiled according to the section. The photograph of the half-section shows that not even the non-coms knew that mounted men wound their puttees from the top down to the ankles. This was not reversed until we reached England. The bandoleers worn in the photograph were of the Canadian type as were also the jackets and caps. These bandoleers had pockets for small arms ammunition in almost a full circle but the British type issued to us in England had pockets only in the front and these held more than we could ever need but they came in handy to hold cigarettes, etc. As our jackets and caps became worn they were replaced by British types, the jacket with double collar and the cap without a wire frame. Our greatcoats will be mentioned later. It will be noticed in the photograph that some wore maple leafs on their collars while others wore grenades. This condition persisted as there was official uncertainty as to whether the artillery should wear grenades which were also worn by the Engineers. Good old war! I also had my photograph taken in Winnipeg which shows me as I felt.

Travelling east

On March 6th we said good-bye to Winnipeg. I had been there such a short time that there was little cause for regret at leaving but a very deep regret that our leaving was arranged so quickly that I could not go home to say good-bye to my family. I tried to arrange that I might leave a day or two earlier and join the unit at Montreal but was not successful. In a driving snowstorm on the night of March 6th we marched down Main Street to the C. P. R. station which had been rebuilt in 1914, and entrained in colonist cars. A large proportion of our men came from farms on the prairies but Winnipeg was well represented so there was quite a rousing farewell for all of us. I can say that with few exceptions it was a congenial group of men.

Next afternoon we came to Fort William and were lined up on the station platform for inspection. I was refused permission to break ranks and speak to a dear friend who had come to the station to wish me luck. The following day, March 8th, we passed through Chapleau and many friends were out to meet John and me. Harry Pelton, Harry Sault, Emma Noel, the Curran sisters, Bill McMullen and many others. We were presented with a bottle of gin and a bottle of whisky each and a warm farewell from all of the girls. Even the officers were friendly that evening, but we formed a close corporation to dispose of the liquor. Our train made a detour around Ottawa and went through Smith's Falls to Montreal where we arrived early on March 9th. Brother Norman was out to meet me and to say good-bye for the family in Turcot Yards where we switched over to the Intercolonial Railway lines. This was before the United States had entered the war and the C. P. R. line through Maine was not available for troop movements of belligerent countries such as Canada. We arrived at Saint John, New Brunswick on Friday night March 10th where we remained in the yards all night and embarked next morning about eight o'clock on the S. S. Metagama. The ship had not been changed when going into the troopship service and four of us were given a regular cabin with two double bunks and white sheets. The food turned out to be the worst part of the service and consisted mostly of tripe and hard-boiled eggs. We left Saint John harbour on Sunday, March 12th, about five in the afternoon and found the Bay of Fundy quite calm. We arrived in Halifax harbour the next afternoon and remained there until the 17th. I had a turn of four hours' guard duty and we had our first inoculation on board here. We left Halifax early on the morning of the 17th—our ship, the S. S. Lapland and a British cruiser, the Carnarvon. We later found that the Lapland had on board troops from Winnipeg who had had no notice of leaving when we left there. This was my first ocean voyage and although the weather was fairly rough I did not experience seasickness. We had church parades, drills, tournaments and entertainments. The other two sections of our Column were on board and also a large number of unattached officers. On March 21st the Carnarvon left us and we were taken over by another cruiser. On the 24th we enjoyed the sight of several destroyers ploughing towards us through the heavy seas. At times it seemed that they had been swamped but they eventually took us into their care and the cruiser went about other business. At about the same time we sighted land which must have been the west coast of Ireland and we were ordered to put on life belts which we wore until we pulled into the Mersey River next afternoon. The U-boat menace was ever-present but not as intense as it would be within a year. We docked at Liverpool at five in the afternoon on Saturday March 25th and disembarked at midnight. After standing about for two hours we

5

entrained in daintily painted cars that reminded me of bird cages and pulled out at three in the morning.

AMMUNITION MEN LEAVE FOR FRONT

Get Hearty Send-off—Big Crowd at the Depot in Spite of the Snowstorm.

Despite the snowstorm which enveloped the city last night, a large crowd of relatives and friends assembled to give the members of the ammunition column a hearty send-off, and they waited patiently to see the last of the train, which pulled out amid ringing cheers.

Long before the time set for the departure of the train, people were making their way to the depot, some on foot, others by street car or jitney, and they were allowed on the platform to say good-bye to their loved ones. A strong military picket furnished by the 53rd, 78th, 100th and 108th Battalions marshalled the crowd and kept a clear path for the departing troops. Capt. Goddard, assistant provost-marshal, was in attendance, and everything passed off without a hitch.

The following officers and men, 173 in number, were included in the party:

Captain Kruger, Lieutenants Miles and Sherlock, Bergt.-Major McFadden, Sergt. Quinn, Sergt. Preston, Corp. Beachem, Corp. Knowles, Corp. Coleman, Shoeing-Smiths Sidders, Hilland, Rorton, McKibben and Campbell, Saddlers Beckett and Williamson, Wheelers Wheeler and Vaughan, Bombs. Clark, Judge, Lees, Keal, Kirby, Cape. R. B. Adam, J. B. Aikenhead, A. Bartlett, A. D. Bannister, S. J. Bartlett, C. H. Brown, F. Clift, W. C. Clifford, A. Chisholm, J. Crabb, A. Cotter, W. K. Farthing, H. Fort, H. Fowler, C. Foster, J. Gibson, A. Gillan, A. A. Gooderick, H. G. Hesler, S. A. Hopp, W. H. Harvey, A. K. Horn, J. E. Hay, Y. Lloyd, S. J. King, O. L. Legge, W. Milford, J. K. Miller, G. A. MacFarlane, C. B. McDougall, W. J. Noble, H. Osmundson, C. Parsons, A. Parkins, S. Perry, F. Pryce, J. Patterson, S. Price, D. Reid, D. C. Scott, W. Shields, D. Sidders, W. R. Squires, G. T. Strange, A. P. Vaughan, D. T. Vaughan, R. Wallace, W. T. Wallace, W. F. Walker, J. Henry Wilkinson, B. J. Wilkinson, F. D. Wilkinson, A. B. Verinder, L. Armin, R. B. Atkinson, W. B. Bulloch, L. B. Beales, E. J. Burr, J. E. Brownell, J. Currie, J. M. Dunbar, B. Dollimore, W. H. Davies, A. Davis, G. Evans, W. Farquharson, H. S. Ford, F. Gartside, F. H. Kean, H. Hicks, M. E. Hogarth, F. Manson, W. Meek, J. A. Mitchell, W. H. Mosley, F. Morley, A. A. Middleton, R. MacDonald, J. McPhail, S. O. Parker, R. C. Parsons, W. Patterson, W. Rombough, G. S. Ramsay, F. P. Sawkins, W. B. Simpson, W. E. Smith, T. Verner, F. H. Verinder, W. E. Vincent, P. F. Wallace, F. Wilson, G. H. Wilson, G. Walker, A. L. Whitlock, E. Welsh, G. J. Wrathall, A. J. S. Wright, A. H. Wilkinson, L. Wantuck, E. D. Alder, R. G. Anderson, H. Baldwin, P. Berry, A. E. Bowman, W. J. Brown, G. H. Beales, R. A. Colier, B. Campbell, G. Davey, G. H. Dolk, W. A. Dixon, J. Davidson, S. M. Ellis, A. W. Gaunt, B. W. Hague, C. Houston, J. Hewitson, O. T. Kay, J. W. Johnson, T. Low, E. V. Lewis, W. G. Luce, P. Murray, R. Mackey, C. R. Marshall, W. Mowatt, B. W. Modeland, D. E. Meloche, A. E. Owens, S. Phips, W. G. Price, W. Parkinson, R. F. A. Redfern, C. H. Sime, J. G. A. Scott, A. Sinclair, L. Stephens, J. A. Thompson, J. Wilkinson, L. Wheeldon, R. Wade, G. J. Whitlock, H. Westberg, F. Vaughan and J. L. Zoller.

EXTRACT FROM THE MANITOBA FREE PRESS
MARCH 7, 1916

Sojourn in the South of England

We arrived at Liphook, Hampshire at 11:30 A.M. on Sunday, March 26th, and from there marched to Bramshott Camp where we settled in huts. In the afternoon we were allowed out of camp on passes and with several companions I went to the attractive nearby village of Hazelmere and sampled the English beer which was then not as watery as it later became. To limber us up we went on a route march the next day to Grayshott and return. On Tuesday, March 28th, we marched many muddy miles to be inspected by the controversial Sir Sam Hughes, Minister of Militia and Defence. Ironically on that same day in Parliament at Ottawa, Sir Sam's administration of his department was being strongly criticized, giving rise to the appointment of a Royal Commission which exonerated him, but he was on the way out. His resignation was called for on November 14th and the department was divided between a representative in London and another in Ottawa. That evening I joined up with Bill Carr from Port Colborne whom I had met in camp and we walked to Grayshott through a driving snow-storm to have a few beers. On March 29th we were inspected by some other general whose name I do not recall.

On Saturday, April 1st, we went on another route march and in the evening I walked to Hazelmere. On Sunday I went to Liphook. On the 3rd the first group to be given six days' leave left camp. Men with relatives in the British Isles were given preference in this form of leave but I was vaccinated that day. The next day I reported sick and was sent to a field hospital with tonsillitis. This immobilized me for a week with much discomfort, as for a few days I could barely swallow water and could get no light food within the army rations except the custard prepared from powder which was to be an almost daily item on our "menus" during our stay in England.

On Thursday, April 13th, my turn came for six days' leave and I went to London where I lodged at the Union Jack Club. Although the Maple Leaf Club had been opened in 1915 and at the time of this visit was being enlarged, it was in the West End and I chose to stay at the Union Jack Club which was near Waterloo Station, the terminal of the railway to and from Surrey. This club was open to members of the Allied forces and I remember being impressed by the size of some Russian soldiers who were there. I spent most of my time sight-seeing; the Tower of London, etc., movies (cinema) and theatres. The people of London were a bit jittery after several recent Zeppelin raids and the black-out was complete. During my absence my unit had moved to Witley Camp. This was somewhat farther into Surrey and near Godalming, whereas Bramshott and the other places previously mentioned were near the point where Surrey, Hampshire and Sussex come together. In the area was the Devil's Punch Bowl and the Gibbet at Hindhead—depressing scenery.

A BREAK DURING BOOT CAMP AT WITLEY, SURREY, JUNE 1916
(DRIVER HESLER IS 3ʳᵈ FROM LEFT, REAR ROW)

Four weeks in England and we were still without animals but that was remedied on Easter Sunday, April 23rd, when we marched to Milford Station and took over some horses and mules. On Easter Monday those free of duty received late passes and I was one of those that went to the nearest city, Guildford, where we heard the news of the Easter rebellion in Ireland.

On Friday, June 2nd, I went to London on week-end pass with two companions and again stayed at the Union Jack Club. During this visit I saw for the first time the changing of the guard at Buckingham Palace where we were cautioned by a burly Sergeant-Major in terms which often caused fistic combat between the British and Canadian troops. Here we had to submit to "mind now, you bloody colonials to salute when the colours pass". The Battle of Jutland had been fought on May 31st and while we were in London discussion was waged in the newspapers and wherever people met as to whether it was a victory or a defeat, and when we were back in camp we heard of the loss of Lord Kitchener on his way to Russia.

Apparently most unit commanders were still expecting activities at the front to change to open warfare. There were rumours amongst the many that circulated of an impending battle of magnitude and our Captain took advantage of the squeamishness of others and traded off our poorest dark-coloured horses for good Greys, so that by the time we passed in review before King George V in July practically all of our horses were Greys. This review was a "farewell" for the Fourth Division infantry and the Third Division Artillery of the Canadian Corps which were to go to the front in August and July respectively. Of the Third Division infantry the 7th and 8th Brigades had been formed in Flanders in December 1915 and included the Princess Pats which had been there for a year. The 9th Brigade was formed in February 1916 when it went to the front.

CANADIAN 18-POUNDER GUN CREW IN TRAINING

While we did not have our full complement of animals and wagons until a few days before we left for the front we had mounted exercises with men taking turns with the animals on hand. A few days before we left I was given a team of grey horses and rode center with W. Brown at the wheel position and Syd Bartlett at the lead, hitched to a limbered ammunition wagon. We usually had Sunday afternoons and evenings off unless detailed for piquet or other duties and on most such occasions walked to Godalming or other nearby towns or villages. One Sunday afternoon Tommy Mitchell and I rented a canoe on the River Wey thus satisfying Canadian nostalgia but causing a fuss when we insisted upon being locked through a passage of falling waters. Before we left England the rules had been changed to allow soldiers to shave their upper lips and away went my wisp of blonde moustache. Also, the left-handed salute was abolished. This had been an awkward manoeuvre for a right-handed man and was called for when passing officers right side to right side. To avoid it we often tried to shift positions to pass right side to left side or in general to go off at a tangent and avoid saluting in any manner. Several officers and N.C.O.'s were assigned to us from other units, one of them being Sergeant Butchers who, I discovered during World War II, was then at the head of the finger-print bureau of the R. C. M. P. in Ottawa. We were both better suited to sedentary jobs than riding horses.

Moving to the Continent

At daybreak on Friday July 14th we set out for Liphook station where we loaded our animals and wagons on railway cars and soon were on our way to Southampton where we boarded ship in the early afternoon. This thing of loading animals on trains and ships was something new to me but our western boys were probably better at it than the officers in charge of such operations. We sailed at 5 P.M. in beautiful summer weather and arrived at Le Havre early next morning. The unloading of stubborn animals was probably more difficult than the loading had been and some of them had to be landed in slings by cranes. Finally assembled we set out through the city streets to a rest camp on a hill overlooking the harbour. This was my first view of France and about the only feature I recall distinctly was the open latrines in the streets. We spent Sunday at the camp and early on Monday, July 17th, set out for the railway yards where we boarded a train made up of those famous box cars marked "8 chevaux - 40 hommes". It was not an uncomfortable trip for those assigned to cars with animals where there was plenty of hay to rest on, but one of the cars was the scene of considerable disturbance when a horse took fright when passing through a tunnel and broke loose. We passed through Rouen, Boulogne, Calais and Saint-Omer and arrived at our destination, Godewaersvelde, on the morning of Tuesday, July 18th. We marched to a farm near the town of Steenvoorde where we arrived in the afternoon. Both of these towns are about 10 to 12 miles west of Ypes and in sight of the Monts de Flandre with their separate upthrusts known as Mont des Cats, Mont Cassel, Mont Noir and Mont Kemmel, similar to those on the south shore of the Saint Lawrence River, east of Montreal. The Steenvoorde area was camping ground for the Canadian Corps whenever they were in the Ypres sector.

We were at this camp for about a week of training and reorganization. Our Sergeant-Major who had come with us from Winnipeg was too old (and crotchety!) to go to the front and was replaced by a somewhat illiterate professional soldier who sometimes scolded us about "putting refuge in the insinuator". Our new senior officer was a Captain Cook, heartily disliked by all including the Sergeant-Major who could not handle the long words used by the Captain in orders. I met Cook again in Havana in 1920 when he was in the Canadian Trade Commission service and he had not changed much. Of the subalterns, the only one I remember was a Lieut. Edgecombe who was a very decent fellow. Over the years we had many changes of officers. If an officer could not hold his own in a battery he was down-graded to us and if he was not good enough for even that he might go to the Trench Mortars. We had been issued with gas-masks, the grey Ku Klux Klan model, which had come into use in November 1915 following the improvised protectors used after the Second Battle of Ypres. It fitted into a small bag carried on a shoulder sling. Later in the year these were replaced by the box respirator. Steel helmets had been brought into use in late 1915 but distribution was slow and we did not receive our full supply until after several weeks. In the meantime the supply was pooled and drawn on by those "going up the line". Weighing about two pounds there was always a temptation to shed them but anyone caught doing so was severely reprimanded. Our move to the front also coincided with the withdrawal of the Ross rifle and the substitution of the Lee Enfield with which our complement of about fifty was filled. This farm was a pleasant spot during the ideal weather which prevailed and with a small stream in which we could bathe we were lulled into a false impression of what our future on the continent was to be.

> WAR DIARY OF THE 3RD DIVISIONAL AMMUNITION COLUMN FOR
> AUGUST 9, 1916:
> Gas attack.   Horses & mules affected—one dying—2 had to be
> shot. 6 men sent to hospital gassed.   Men now have confidence in gas
> helmets.   One man killed, stray bullet.

After nearly a week of shake-down exercises we left here on Monday, July 24th and moved a few miles across the border into Belgium to a camp before Poperinghe, just off the main road to Ypres. The people on the farm here were not very gracious and a few incidents arose during our month's stay in which we had our first experiences of night-time trips to the gun positions. Such trips usually included a passage through the dreaded spot of Hell Fire Corner. On Friday, August 25th, we returned to the old camp near Steenvoorde for a "rest". I was ill for several days and thereby escaped the general punishment which Captain Cook imposed on the section for some trivial incident. At about this time Divisional markings on clothing and vehicles were introduced and we were made busy sewing oblong patches on our sleeves at the shoulders and stencilling red dumb-bells on our vehicles. From this latter insignia there arose the name of the well-known concert party formed from within the 3rd Division—"The Dumb-Bells". The shoulder patches were at first black but there were such strong objections to this depressing badge that it was soon changed to French grey. The First Division markings were red patches and I believe their vehicle markings were the same but the 2nd Division wore dark blue patches and for vehicles they had a large "C" with two vertical bars in the arc. The 4th Division which had no artillery at the front at that time chose a green shoulder patch and a maple leaf for vehicles.

HELLFIRE CORNER, NEAR YPRES

On Wednesday, September 6th, we moved to a point on the border between Locre and Bailleul, behind Kemmel Hill. On Saturday the 9th we moved back into France about two miles to Croix de Poperinghe, near Bailleul. We were now getting a foretaste of what life would be like in wet weather but it was nothing compared to what we would go through during our next sojourn in these parts in late 1917 in the Passchendaele battles. Bailleul was an attractive and busy city not far behind the lines then but it was completely destroyed in March 1918. My military life was almost interrupted here one day when, on a trip to the railhead for supplies, my horse fell on me while going over slippery cobblestones but I came out of it with only a bruised leg. During this period I made my first trips to the front line trenches at Kemmel in connection with the trench mortars. The farm where we were camped was a dismal place but it provided my first view of hop vines and the hop gatherers on stilts. The beer made from these hops was very watery. In this shuttling back and forth across the border between France and Belgium we passed by the "Duanes" (customs houses) which still operated for civilians. When I crossed the border as a civilian in 1938 the customs examinations were little more than they had been for us as soldiers and that was nothing.

> WAR DIARY OF THE 3RD DIVISIONAL AMMUNITION COLUMN FOR
> DECEMBER 11, 1916:
> Working Party of 90 men sent to Trench Mortars near Maroeuil
> during night.

When the 3rd Divisional Artillery and the 4th Division infantry went to the front in July and August 1916 the Canadian Corps, which had been placed under the command of Sir Julian Byng in May of that year, was still in the Ypres area where there then was little activity after the strenuous fighting at Sanctuary Wood during the first part of June which had caused many Canadian casualties and inroads on reserves, disrupting to some extent the organization of the 4th Division. The French had taken the offensive at Verdun in February and there was great activity there until September. The British had opened their offensive on the Somme on July 1st but it was not until the first days of September that the Canadians were brought into the lines there when the 1st Division relieved the Australians and they were followed by the 2nd and 3rd Divisions, the latter being supported by a division of British Field Artillery. This move was part of Haig's plan for a big new offensive battle to begin on September 15th. On that day the Canadians made some headway and captured Courcelette, a village which was destroyed in the process of the battle over dry ground. When we reached the Somme area a month later Courcelette and Martinpuich, separated by the Albert-Bapaume road, were not distinguishable as villages in the sea of mud which had been churned up in the rainy fall weather which ensued.

On October 1st these three divisions took part in a new offensive in which their part was to capture Regina trench. Then the rains came and after about two weeks the attack petered out with only some small gains to show for the effort. During this period the 3rd Divisional Artillery and the 4th Division infantry were moving from the Ypres area to the Somme and this was to be the first of our several long treks during the remainder of the war – that is, long in terms of a horse-drawn formation.

The Somme

We set out at 7:30 A.M. from Croix de Poperinghe on Tuesday, October 3rd, and made a little better than 20 miles that day through Merville to Burbure, a couple of miles south of Lillers. The next day we travelled south-west away from the front for about 12 miles to Anvin on the Terroise River. On Thursday we made a similar distance southward to Conchy-sur-Canche, by-passing the important rail-head of Saint-Pol. On Friday the 6th we turned south-eastward through Doullens and camped at Authieule, on the Authie River. On Saturday, October 7th, we travelled along a main road running south-east and came to a camp at Orville behind Albert where we remained two days. At the overnight stops shelter for the men was sometimes improvised by slanting a tarpaulin over a support to accommodate six or eight men but in the rear areas a barn or other building was often available. Sunny France at this time of year was far from bright weather-wise and if we could be glad at all we were glad that we were in a mounted unit as each driver had two saddle blankets which could be used for greater warmth by a driver, as I was, or shared with a non-driver, the latter category making up about one-third of the establishment. As an added benefit it was claimed that saddle blankets which had been on horses or mules were lice repellents but in my experience, which began soon after we arrived on the continent, that was a myth. During our few days outside Albert our shelters were improvised as will be seen in the accompanying photograph. Although I am in this picture I had forgotten that it had been taken until I ran across it during the 1930's in a series of pamphlets "Twenty Years After" which were edited by General Swinton, the inventor of the tank.

ARTILLERYMEN AT ORVILLE, OCTOBER 1916
FOREGROUND, LEFT TO RIGHT: DRIVERS FARTHERING, PARKINSON, HESLER,
PATTERSON, LEGG AND RUMBAUGH
MAN IN REAR IN DARK SWEATER: SGT. GEORGE WILSON

On Tuesday, October 10th, we moved through Albert past the church with the steeple top figure of the Virgin leaning over us at right angle. Just beyond the city we made camp on high ground near the Ancre River opposite the village of Aveluy. We made fairly comfortable shelters for ourselves here and became adept at making stoves out of five gallon oil drums. Our ground was fairly solid but watering the animals was a dirty task as the river bank was a quagmire. Here for the first time we saw some of the tanks that had been too hastily introduced into battle in September and were now lying derelict.

The 4th Division infantry had arrived at about the same time which coincided with a lull in the fighting but preparations were under way for a new offensive in which that division would take part to the exclusion of the other three infantry divisions which withdrew from the area on October 17th. The 4th Division infantry and the 1st, 2nd and 3rd Divisional Artillery became part of the II Corps. In preparation for the operation which began on October 21st, and continuations of it, we were "up the line" every night and sometimes during the daytime. In the first action Regina Trench was captured and November 18th Desire Trench was taken. Shortly after that the 1916 activities on the Somme came to an end.

IMPROVISED SLINGS FOR THE MUD OF THE SOMME

At first we made a few trips to the gun positions in the orthodox manner with limbered ammunition wagons drawn by six horses but the ground was becoming more churned up each day by enemy shelling and frequent and heavy rains. I recall an occasion when we had twelve horses hitched to a wagon but could not drag it through the mud even when unlimbered and with men at the wheels. We improvised slings and packed the ammunition on the backs of the horses to the guns. Upon our return to the camp our saddlers were put to work making slings fashioned out of tarpaulin canvas which fitted over the saddle or bare back of horses and mules and held eight 18-pounder or four 4.5 shells. These slings soon became an army issue and the use of wagons was discontinued when mud made their passage difficult. These slings were used again at Vimy Ridge to some extent and almost exclusively at Passchendaele. On the Somme we would slosh our way out to the main Albert-Bapaume road from which sometimes we would branch off to the right on a minor road at La Boiselle, where a huge crater had been formed on July 1st, and go on through Contalmaison to the neighbourhood of Martinpuich. At other times we would go straight through Pozières and then enter the sea of mud on the left in the neighbourhood of Courcelette. There was little left of any of these villages. I travelled along this Albert-Bapaume road again in 1938 and it was still dismal territory but nothing like it was in November 1916.

> WAR DIARY OF THE 3RD DIVISIONAL AMMUNITION COLUMN FOR
> OCTOBER 23, 1916:
> Dull & cold. Rain during night—Horse lines are now a quagmire,
> mud everywhere over foot deep. Sections all employed during day
> and night as working parties and carrying ammunition to battery
> gun positions. No 2 Section carried 610 rounds to 11th Brigade gun
> positions by means of strapping 4 ammunition baskets on each side
> of saddle as shell holes & roads too bad otherwise.

We had earned the privilege of the rum ration when we first came
to the Continent and it was now increased in frequency but there were
still some teetotallers in the unit who did not imbibe this medicated
firewater. However, they always drew their ration and either sold it
immediately to comrades or hoarded it for a higher market. One late
afternoon the word was passed that we would not be going up the line
that night and the regular rum ration was ladled out. The hoarders now
cashed in on an avid market amongst those who felt a need to celebrate
this first reprieve from the mud fields of the forward area. By the time
an emergency call came in about eight o'clock to rush ammunition to
the guns, a half-dozen or so were in no state to walk, let alone mount or
lead a horse or mule, and next day's field trials brought varying degrees
of punishment, one or two receiving the highest, F. P. No. 1, of being
tied to a wagon wheel twice a day and others were given pack drill.
There was however, a humorous note when we sober ones were on our
way along the main road. A grey horse came galloping from the rear
with the rider shouting "follow me, men, I will lead you into Germany
and we will capture the Kaiser". He was restrained and taken back to
camp. Corporal Bill Shields, a western cowboy who usually held his
liquor well, became Driver Shields after next morning's trial.

> WAR DIARY OF THE 3RD DIVISIONAL AMMUNITION COLUMN FOR
> OCTOBER 28, 1916:
> No 1 Section whilst carrying ammunition to the 8th & 9th Brigades
> were heavily shelled by German Fire near the outskirts of Martinpuich.
> Casualties were: Killed 1 Sgt and 1 other rank; wounded Lieut.
> Hughson and 12 other ranks.

While we were not fighting soldiers in the sense of personal combat, the inhuman conditions of trudging through the fields of mud around and through water-filled shell holes, dragging one or two reluctant animals behind us, with no cover from enemy shelling was frustrating, yet within such category our tasks were probably easier than those of stretcher-bearers. At this time we still had our Canadian great-coats which were splendid protection for the knees while the wearer was in the saddle but coming to within four inches of the ground they were impediments when walking through the mud as one stepped on the long skirt from step to step up and down muddy inclines. One night I became so worn out by such struggles that, regulations or no regulations, I took out my knife and hacked away the surplus cloth but it did not tear well and ended up by being a comfortable length to the knees at the front while it barely covered my seat in the rear. This is what probably saved me from punishment for damaging the King's property as it did not look deliberate and I was able to satisfy inquiries by stating that it had been torn in disentangling myself from barbed wire. It must have been an odd sight however for on our way north shortly afterwards we were standing dismounted in the streets of Aubigny, near a military hospital and some nurses burst into gales of laughter when they saw me. Not long afterwards I obtained my first British-warm, a natty officer type overcoat, which we wore during the winter months for the remainder of the war. It did not cover the knees but a friend of mine in Canada sent me a pair of hip rubber boots which served me well for the next couple of years.

The move to Vimy

Towards the end of November the 4th Division infantry and the three divisions of artillery withdrew from the area and headed north to the Vimy area where we were to be stationed for the next eighteen months, except for the Passchendaele excursion at the end of 1917. We left our camp in front of Albert on Sunday, the 26th, and being the greenest of the artillery troops, had to take our turn in getting on to the one road through Albert and the main road from there to Doullens. Travelling about 16 miles we did not make camp until 10 P.M. at Orville, a few miles south-east of Doullens. The next day we travelled north about ten miles to Estrée Wamin and from there on the following day, November 28th, about 12 miles to Villers Brulin, west of Aubigny. On Friday, December 2nd, we moved through Aubigny for a short distance to Frevin Capelle where we remained for several weeks in huts and covered stables. As a matter of comparison, the total distance travelled by our unit was about 38 miles while in a straight line the distance was 25 miles; the 3rd Division infantry which left Albert on October 10th covered about 60 miles in arriving at about the same destination but they made a wide sweep to the west of Doullens while we kept to the east of that city. We were on the road for three days of uninterrupted travel but they were on the way 12 days with 6 days of rest at three different points. At this time we were joined for the first time to our infantry division, relieving the Lahore Division which had been supporting the 3rd Division and now went to the 4th Canadian Division. Afterwards this division was often in our neighbourhood and it was interesting to observe the way of life of these good Indian troops. Low-minded of me perhaps to be interested for one thing in their manner of brushing their teeth with a green twig and also the delicate poise of steel helmets on turbaned heads.

On Thursday, December 7th, I became one of a party of about a dozen men detailed to do some work for the Trench Mortar batteries. We spent the night at Maroeuil and next day took up quarters in the cellar of a non-existent house in Sainte-Catherine where the road from Arras to Lens branches off. It was here that I "celebrated" my 23rd birthday. Every day for a week we trudged through a communication trench to the front line running just beyond Écurie and Roclincourt, and worked on building a trench mortar emplacement ahead of the front line at a point where the German line was only yards away. On the day we finished our task by installing the mortar and bringing up ammunition which was a steel globe about the size of a basketball filled with explosives and with a steel shaft about twenty inches long, our hosts honoured us by firing a few ranging shots and then we withdrew a short distance to observe any reaction. Within a few minutes we could see "minnies" flying through the air and with a few direct hits all of our work was undone and we returned to our unit at Frevin Capelle. Here we celebrated our first Christmas and New Years at the front and many of the men imbibed a little more freely of the wine and beer at the *estaminets* in the village which bordered our camp. Hereabouts most of the farmers lived in the village and went daily to and from their farms nearby.

CAPTURED GERMAN 17CM MINENWERFER MORTAR, OR "MINNI"

CHAPTER TWO

1917

On Monday January 22nd we moved a few miles from Frévin Capelle to Cambligneul where the animals had to stand in the open and the men found shelter in barn lofts. While we were here this section of France experienced the coldest winter in many years and as some bright officer had put through an order that all animals must be clipped, except for their legs, a number of them died from exposure and many were sent to the base to recuperate. Amongst the latter was Bang of my team of Bing and Bang and I went down the social scale by being allotted a team of mules—but they were good mules of a copper colour and I found that they were more intelligent than most horses. We were here for nearly a month with occasional trips up the line on a very quiet front. About the middle of February the 3rd Division was withdrawn from the line to receive training for the Battle of Vimy, forming part of what the British called the Battle of Arras. We left Camblignuel on Saturday, February 17th, and moved north to Calonne Riquart, near Bruay, in the coal mining area. We did not do much training but were kept busy cleaning harness and grooming animals.

Due to casualties at the Somme and other changes we now had several new officers and non-coms who had been transferred from other units. Our sergeant-major was a young man from Montreal of more bombast than wit but Captain Hendy, our senior officer was a professional soldier, splendid horseman and a good soldier. The new sergeant in my sub-section was George Wilson, a graduate of Ontario Agricultural College, and being fellow Ontarioites we were on friendly terms but our friendship was strained by my abhorrence of harness cleaning. The harness with its breast collars had many brass buckles and steel rings and quick-release connectors, the one metal becoming dull quickly and the other rusting overnight unless greased. The leather also had to be dubbined and the saddles and bridles polished. To clean the steel one had to forage for, and closely guard, a strap to go around the waist on which there was a hooked ring with which to engage the piece of harness to be worked on while the piece was attached to a wall or post. Then with a piece of cloth, not easily come by unless one took a strip off of his shirt tail, moistened and dipped in sand (some officer could always find some sand even where the earth was nothing but gooey mud) the driver would scour the metal. The breaking point between George Wilson and me came when we were ordered to do a special job of polishing for an inspection by General Lipsett, the Divisional Commander. George was fretting all morning about the condition of my harness and was in a dither when the General stopped by my team and asked me where I hailed from. Knowing that he had commanded the 8th Battalion, Winnipeg Rifles, I replied that I came from Winnipeg, which was true in a certain sense. He then complimented me on the condition of my golden mules and the sheen of the harness which they bore. George and I remained good friends and after the war I saw him several times which is more than the occasions on which I saw others of the unit. He became a senior official in the Ontario Department of Agriculture. However, he put the screws on me after the inspection mentioned by switching me to another team of mules and detailing us as part of a small group to join others from the Column to haul material on the light railway at Vimy Ridge.

The Battle of Vimy Ridge

On March 6th our party with its mules went back a few miles to Nédon to help move the 30th Battery to Estrée Couchy the next day. From there we travelled light to Ecoivres, near Mont-Saint-Éloi, where we joined the 4th Section of the Column in a camp of muddy horse lines and dingy huts. One of the mules assigned to me was a perverse animal of strange appearance which delighted in rolling in the mud and kicking anything in range. Somewhere, sometime, when I was not around a photographer was attracted by the unusual animal and took his picture which appeared in R. H. Mottram's *Journey to the Western Front*, published in 1936 and included here. I was ordered to break him down by hard work but although my riding crop was a pick handle he survived the tough period prior to the Battle of Vimy on the light railway.

ONE OF DRIVER HESLER'S MULES AT VIMY RIDGE, APRIL 1917

This light railway of about 24-inch gauge began at a dump in the woods opposite Mont-Saint-Éloi and ran parallel to the road leading to Neuville-Saint-Vaast and then turned north into the communication trenches near the Pimple. Behind La Targette a line branched off to the field gun emplacements and was called the "Inner Circle" while the longer line was called the "Outer Circle". The Inner Circle was used sometimes in daylight but the other could only be used at night and when we got to the end of that line each driver had to stand over his mule and be ready to prevent him from hee-hawing to the Germans not far away. The railway was operated on strict union lines—the drivers did not lift a hand to load or unload the ammunition (field gun and small arm), food, barbed wire and every other class of material that went up the line. The mules were hooked in single file teams of from three to six animals, depending on the weight of the cargo carried. After the battle this railway and others were kept in operation but the cars were pulled by gasoline powered cars.

MULE TEAM DRAWING AMMUNITION ON THE INNER CIRCLE NEAR VIMY, APRIL 1917

It was humdrum work but there was a certain amount of independence in it. We were free to a considerable extent from officers and non-coms. The Lieutenant in charge of the dump was dubbed "Puss-in-Boots". He always wore rubber boots and in his isolated hut must have been lonesome, for more than once he came out of his castle to halt a departing train and caress a mule with the explanation "I love mules". We were close to civilians in the neighbouring towns and the Paris edition of the *London Daily Mail* brought us news. Events reported were the withdrawal of the Germans to the Hindenburg Line on March 14th, the beginning of the Russian Revolution and the declaration of war by the United States on April 6th and by Cuba, a country of little interest to me then, on April 7th. Two other events remain in my memory. One morning at daybreak I was alone on piquet watching over the mules when a German plane came into view over the nearby ruined tower at Mont-Saint-Éloi flying from the east at a very low altitude. The pilot leaned out of his cockpit and gave me a wave of the arm and I recognized the face and plane of Richthoffen. The other event occurred one morning when we were delivering ammunition to batteries on the

Inner Circle. We were sitting on our mules in front of the guns which had been quiet when we arrived and should have been kept that way while their men were unloading our cars. Suddenly they began to fire and I was struck by the look of amazement on the face of one of the drivers on another team—the head of his mule had been cleanly sheared off by a defective shell. Something like a chicken, the mule remained standing for a minute or two. We were using a lot of American-made ammunition at this time and much of it was defective. Even we heard rumours of sabotage in the United States and many artillery men were nervous about using ammunition made there. Another event was the shelling of Mont-Saint-Éloi and surrounding camps on March 24th and 25th but we suffered no damage.

CANADIAN AMMUNITION DRIVERS NEAR VIMY, APRIL, 1917

The opening of the Battle of Vimy (Arras) was set for the morning of April 9th, Easter Monday. On the night of the 8th-9th I had been up to the end of the Outer Circle and did not get back to the lines until about 3 A.M. so when the barrage started at 5:30 I, somewhat like a general having given his final orders, just rolled over and wished them luck. The weather was bad with sleet and snow but the battle moved forward without any further help from us. On Wednesday April 11th it was snowing rather heavily and I think it was on this day that my mule was photographed as it will be seen that there was snow on the ground at his feet. Members of our Section were up the line that day and on their way back picked us up and guided us through a heavy blizzard to our lines which were then at Barlin, south of Béthune. On Saturday, April 14th, we moved about five miles south to Petit Servins. The next day I had an interesting experience when about a dozen of us, mounted on single mules, trekked about 10 miles to the old gun positions, near La Targette, to pick up ammunition and move it forward. There a problem arose because the ammunition was to be delivered to two batteries located in different directions and there was only one non-com, Sergeant De Ath. He solved it by delegating me to take charge of half of the group in a speech which must have been recalled from his history lessons of the time of Queen Elizabeth and Drake and cautioning me that we were to make only one trip and return to Petit Servins before dark. My little group loaded up their packs and moved out over ground which was now drying out but still held uncollected corpses of men killed on April 9th. The plank road connecting the Arras-Béthune and Arras-Lens roads which we later used had not been built and we went across country through obliterated Neuville-Saint-Vaast and then down the sloping road on the east side of the escarpment into Vimy village from which the Germans had retired on April 13 and was then occupied by our field gun batteries. Here we delivered the loads while the Germans started up a strafe of the gun positions. The Battery Sergeant-Major tried to persuade me to bring in another load and during our argument I ordered my men to pull out and wait for me at the top of the ridge. The Sergeant-Major tried to pull rank on me but I bested him in verbal combat and set out on my lone return journey. Fritz must have seen my group going up the incline and by the time I got there he was shelling the road in a moving pattern which accompanied me most of the way but my mule was fast, and probably as frightened, as I was, and we outran the range.

On Saturday, April 21st, we moved to a new camp in front of Mont-Saint-Éloi and behind Berthonval Farm, commonly known as B. Farm, in an area now free from ground observation by the enemy but holding a large concentration of horse lines and a new airdrome on our right, all of which attracted some bombing. This airdrome consisted of a bumpy sloping field edged by a row of gleaming white tents in which the small planes were sheltered. We were kept fairly busy but there was time for horse shows and sports events and also a spate of horse-trading between units in the area which at times was one-sided if any unit became careless and allowed any of their animals to stray. At one time we had about 15 animals in excess of the establishment for which we were allowed to draw rations. In this situation the Captain was tipped off that the Divisional Commander would be paying us a visit and men were detailed to take these excess animals away from camp and let them loose. They could not have taken them far for during the visit, feeding time arrived and shortly after the bugle blew the signal for placing nose-bags, these orphans trotted innocently into their places in our lines. Our Captain got away with it but that night the men who went up the line each took one of these animals with him and let it loose beyond the ridge.

During the month of June 1917 there was an extensive reorganization of the Canadian Corps. General Sir Arthur Currie was appointed to command it, the 4th Divisional Artillery was formed out of units from the other three divisions in the field and, in anticipation, the original 4th Divisional Artillery, still in England, had been reorganized into two brigades and renamed the 5th Divisional Artillery, in February.

As part of this reorganization, Divisional Artillery was changed from 4 Brigades, each with 4 Batteries of 4 guns each, with a total of 64 guns. After reorganization each division, 1st to 5th inclusive, had 2 Brigades each, consisting of 3 six-gun batteries of 18 pounders and 1 six-gun battery of 4.5 howitzers to each brigade, making a total of 48 guns in each division. In addition the 8th Army Brigade was formed by existing batteries of the 3rd Division of 18-pounders and 4.5's, totalling 24 guns. The Divisional Ammunition Columns were reduced from 4 to 3 Sections and one Section from each divisional unit went to form the 4th Canadian Divisional Ammunition Column.

The new 4th Divisional Artillery consisted of:
    3rd Brigade, C.F.A. (from the 1st Division)
        9th Battery - Howitzer
        10th "   - 18-pounder
        11th "   -   "
        12th "   -   "
    4th Brigade, C.F.A. (from the 2nd Division)
        13th Battery - 18-pounder
        19th "   -   "
        21st "   - Howitzer
        27th "   - 18-pounder
    4th Canadian Divisional Ammunition Column, C.F.A.
        Sections Numbers 1, 2 and 3. (One Section
        from each of 1st, 2nd and 3rd Canadian
        Divisional Ammunition Columns).

Under this reorganization we, No. 3 Section, 3rd Canadian Divisional Ammunition Column became No. 2 Section, 4th Canadian Divisional Ammunition Column. One of our men who had been called to be a member of "The Dumbells" remained with the 3rd Division. We had lost another man from Winnipeg, Fred Parsons, who was drafted to do police work in Mesopotamia because of his boxing ability. His father was still with us at the time. We acquired a new section commander, Captain Shaw, of Montreal, as big, physically as General Currie. Our new Colonel was Colonel Gillmore, who the same as his predecessor, Colonel Hurdman, came from Ottawa. There was a small group in our section which included Tees, who became a Brigadier in 1942, and Johnson, the well-known "Ching" star defenceman of the New York Rangers hockey club in later years, who had earlier dubbed us "Hurdman's Hungry Hussars" so now alliteratively we became "Gillmore's Galloping Gazooks". I met with Ching in Montreal several times in the 1930's when his hockey playing career was coming to an end and I was glad to read in recent newspaper reports that he is still active in the world of sports.

Under our new designation we moved on June 25th from before Mont-Saint-Éloi to Bouvigny Woods. On the 28th the 3rd and 4th Divisions began an offensive which was successful in pushing the line closer to the city of Lens which was straight ahead of us. Bouvigny

Woods was at the western end of a spur running into the Souchez Valley, west of Lens, from which the Germans had been dislodged in 1915 by the costly French offensive of that time. As at Mont-Saint-Éloi, we were again with open horse lines and bivouacs constructed by the men. With a team-mate, Dick Coller, I shared a small abode which we had built out of scrap material with chicken-wire cots making a comfortable shelter in the pleasant summer weather. We were not far from the villages of Gouy and Gouy Servins and had the amenities of daily newspaper delivery and a good camp canteen. I recall a pleasant day spent on a trip to a town some distance in the rear where we replenished our beer supply. I also recall the excitement of watching a British firing party march into the woods with a pair of convicted men and listening to the ensuing salvo of execution. Also that there was an abundant crop of wild strawberries to be freely gathered and to be eaten with fresh milk not so freely gathered from cows which the farmers allowed to stray in grazing. I do not recall that we had more than a few church parades, many fewer than our marches to the baths, during the time we were at the front. We had one here at Bouvigny Woods when oddly there was a chaplain attached to the Column. He was very young and had his finger in every pie including the horse thieving between units which was carried on from time to time.

One of our first tasks as part of the 4th Division was to change the Divisional signs on all of our vehicles from the 3rd Division dumb-bell to the 4th Division Maple Leaf and the French grey patches at our shoulders to dark green ones. There was delay in the latter as I notice that the jacket which I wore in Paris in August had no patches—maybe it was a new one and I did not have time for sewing. The 5th Divisional Artillery which came to France in August wore a purple shoulder patch and their vehicles bore a large "C" with five horizontal stripes in the arc. We received some additions to the strength of our unit by way of slightly trained recruits bearing numbers up in the millions and therefore referred to as box-cars which was unfair as at that time the numbers were not closely related to the time of enlistment. One of these men was the cause of the only scar I carried for years as a result of war service. I was helping him to mount a horse without a saddle when he lashed out with one leg and dealt me a gash above an eye with his steel-plated heel.

On Sunday, July 8th, I was detailed as one of the second party from our unit of about 15 men despatched to Boulogne to pick up animals at the remount depot there. With a saddle and two bridles each we were transported to Béthune in wagons and from there travelled by train to the coast where we arrived early on Monday and had most of the day free in Boulogne. The next day we went to the remount depot where I failed in a dodge attempted in the hope that there would not be enough animals at two per man to go around. I was left with the two poorest animals in the lot! One was an entirely unbroken mule which could not be saddled and the other was a huge old grey mule about 16½ hands high. Mounted on the latter and dragging the other I formed up with the others and we set off at 4 P.M. We covered about 12 miles before stopping overnight at a staging camp at Desvres. Travelling all day on Wednesday, July 11th, we camped overnight near Aire and on our way caught our first glimpse of Portuguese artillery units which was not inspiring. The next day we ended our journey at Calonne Ricouart where we had spent part of the previous winter, and left our charges in a distribution depot there. We spent the night at the depot and on Friday, July 13th, were transported to our lines.

Lens

We made frequent trips up the line, increasing in activity in the preparation and support of the attack on Hill 70 near Lens which began on August 15 and ended with capture on the 25th. During this period one trip had varied consequences. As one of a party with about four ammunition wagons I made a trip after dark to our guns in Lieven, a suburb of Lens, and while there we were subjected to a bombardment of gas shells poured into the remains of buildings surrounding us. Shortly before this gas masks had been distributed for use on horses and mules with unusually humane instructions that the men were to don their own masks first in case of need. However, with that impediment over one's face it was quite a struggle to place masks properly on two mules and there was risk of displacement of the man's mask in doing so and the inhalation of gas. Getting back to our lines in the early morning I availed myself of the standing arrangement for such cases and missed morning stable parade. When I turned out during the morning I discovered that all other members of the party had reported on the sick call and all of them had been sent to base hospital with gas effects. I felt no symptoms and I am sure that most of the others were similarly free but they won a good holiday. Nevertheless I reported for a medical examination next day and was declared free of any ill effects. As compensation I was offered immediate leave to Paris which had been opened up to Canadian service men that year, provided I dropped to the end of the list for leave to Blighty which then seemed far in the distance anyway.

On leave in Paris

I accepted the proposal and on Wednesday, August 29th, set out from Bouvigny Woods on a horse accompanied by one of our men who was to bring my mount back from Houdain where I boarded a passenger train at 11 A.M. bound for Saint-Pol. There at 2:30 I changed trains and did the same at Amiens at 6:30, arriving in Paris at 9 in the evening. Sergeant Wilson had been in Paris on leave and he suggested that I stay at the Hôtel de Malte at 63 Rue Richelieu, behind the Palais Royal. It provided comfortable quarters and seemed luxurious after over a year of primitive habitations. I looked it over in 1938 and was not so favourably impressed although a guide book of that time listed it as "excellent".

The next morning I reported to the Military Police and at their suggestion dropped in at the Corner of Blighty on Place Vendome, a small club room set up by the British. Standing in Place Vendome at noon I was surprised by a touch on the shoulder and an English query "well Canada, where to now?". That way I met Mr. Nightingale who was in charge of the French branch of an English firm of wallpaper manufacturers. He suggested that we have a bite to eat and led me to Les Halles Centrales, not far away, the famous market of Paris, where we picked up some lamb chops and vegetables and took them to the neighbouring Café Michel where he turned over the food to be cooked and then we had a good meal. He lived outside Paris and suggested that I meet him later at the station, Gare du Quai d'Orsay where he would show me around Hotel d'Orsay and, as far as possible, Palais d'Orsay. This I did, but in the meantime I met up with a French soldier who had been a guide for Cooks and over a beer or two he gave me useful information for later excursions.

The next day I made limited forays, Tuileries and such places, and on Saturday I joined a party leaving from the Y. M. C. A. on a *char-à-bancs* tour of the city which lasted for most of the day and took in all of the usual tourist points. On the morning of Sunday, September 2nd I walked around Île de la Cité and Île Saint-Louis and took in Notre Dame Cathedral, then to Quai d'Orsay, or Orléans, station where about noon I boarded a train and rode for 12 miles to Ablon on the far side of the Seine where Mr. Nightingale met me. We went to his home surrounded by a pleasant garden and had a good lunch. His family was living in London and we had the place to ourselves. In the afternoon we strolled across the bridge and visited some of his friends, mostly French, in Villeneuve-Saint-Georges. When told that I was a Canadian one lady expressed amazement that I was white. A very pleasant day.

ON LEAVE IN PARIS, SEPTEMBER 1917

On Monday, September 3rd, while Canadians at home would be celebrating a war-time Labour Day, I joined a party and visited Versailles. Maintenance was at a minimum and while impressive if wasteful, it was not as resplendent then as it was in 1938 when I visited it again in the midst of many German tourists.

On the 4th I covered a large part of the city by myself and became acquainted with the *Métropolitain* (subway) and took time to have my picture taken for the folks back home. Next day I went out to Bois de

Boulonge and Auteuil and Longchamps race-courses. I ended my tours on the morning of Thursday, September 6th in Montmartre and in the afternoon went to the Opéra Comique to see *"Le Roi Lys"*. There was a capacity attendance, mostly civilian, and a long line before the ticket window which was being kept in order by a buxom lady. When she caught sight of me away down the line she came and pulled me out and up to the window and ordered the attendant to give me a ticket gratis and I found that it was in a good location. I left from Gare du Nord at 10 P.M. and arrived at Calonne Ricouart about 10 A.M. on Sunday, September 9th. After a bite to eat I set out from there and taking the old Roman road through Houdain walked to Bouvigny Woods about 10 miles, where I arrived at 5:30 P.M. There was little traffic on the road and few opportunities for hitch-hiking, an unknown word at that time, but not an unusual practice, but I did not mind the effort after those ten days of a different life.

Passchendaele

The 3rd Battle of Ypres had been under way since July 31st but, except for the action by the Canadian Corps at Hill 70 and Lens, August 15-25, we had kept on in our hum-drum way in the Lens-Vimy area until Tuesday, October 9th, when we moved from Bouvigny Woods to nearby Gouy Servins. On October 12th we left Gouy Servins and travelled 10 miles to Vendin, near Béthune. The next day we went through Saint-Vinant and the western part of Nieppe Forest covering 12 miles to Morbecque, south of Hazebrouck. By this time there was no doubt that the earlier news via the grapevine was correct, we were headed for Ypres. On Sunday the 14th we passed through Hazebrouck, an important railway junction, and in my memory a pleasant town because we had the unusual experience of the townspeople plying us with apples and other fruit as we stood at rest in their streets. It was badly damaged in the German advance in the Spring of 1918 but was not captured. After we left this city we became more aware of the damp weather and the swampy ground which was to burden us during the next few weeks. After a short haul of 9 miles that day we came to familiar ground near Steenvoorde where we had been initiated in July of 1916. On Monday, October 15th, we moved forward about 11 miles to open horse lines and makeshift billets near Vlamertinge. This area was now blanketed with horselines and other camps, many more than in 1916, and the wet ground was churned up by countless hoofs of horses and mules. The Canadian infantry did not arrive in the forward area until October 22nd but we began immediately to prepare for the impending battle to capture Passchendaele Ridge.

GERMAN PRISONERS BEING MARCHED INTO YPRES
AS MULESKINNERS MOVE TO THE FRONT

Our route to the guns lay through the city of Ypres where we picked up ammunition and packed it on the backs of two mules or horses per man. Although the city had been further levelled since we were last here and the sogginess of the area behind it was disheartening the view as one emerged from the eastern side of the city, through Menin Gate, and crossed the moat-like stream, was one of utmost destruction with nothing but seas of mud and water being continually churned by enemy shells, their explosions adding to the din of our own guns, beginning with 15-inch pieces near the city walls. The eastern exit from the city had been marked by stone lions before the war and was known as the Menin Gate which is now represented by a memorial arch erected by the British in 1927 and dedicated to the hosts of British dead in this area. It survived the later war in which the troops passed by quickly in both directions. While the seas of mud still remain in my memory my sympathy went out to those Canadians who fought along the coast of Holland in the Battle of the Scheldt in the Fall of 1944. Outside the city a road branches off to the right to pass by Hell-fire Corner, Hooge and Sanctuary Wood on the way to the small town of Menin. The left branch goes on to Zonnebeke and from its farther extension a branch road runs to Passchendaele and points northward. I passed along these latter roads in 1938 when every field was green but the ground was still uneven and piles of raked-up shells and other war debris still remained, not as reminders, for anyone having seen this area in 1917 needs no reminder of its ghastly devastation.

WAR DIARY OF THE 4TH DIVISIONAL AMMUNITION COLUMN FOR OCTOBER 20, 1917: 1 OR killed by shell fire near Ypres. 3 OR evacuated to Hospital, shell gas. Vicinity wagon lines bombed by hostile air craft, from 7-pm to 10-pm.

The first assault was made on October 26th by the 3rd and 4th Divisions but little headway was made. On the 28th I, along with several others, was sent off with our teams and wagons to join a Mobile Brigade of British Artillery for purposes which I never knew and never discovered for next day, without having performed any duty, we were sent back to our unit holding a feeling of relief that we would not have to subsist on the smaller rations of the Brigade, or at least those that they doled out to us. The next phase of the assault was carried out by the same divisions on October 30-31 and the ridge was carried. On November 6th the 1st and 2nd Divisions captured the village of Passchendaele and the work of the Canadian Corps in this area began to peter out.

PACK MULES PASS BY A WRECKED ARTILLERY LIMBER
NEAR YPRES, 31 JULY 1917

During this period we carried out various classes of duties but the worst was taking ammunition up the line. The main road was kept in fair repair up to a point where concentrated shelling broke it up. Beyond that, and off to the sides, the soft earth was honey-combed with water-filled shell holes and it was a neat balancing feat to find one's way at night through this maze, dragging two loaded mules behind, to a gun pit, particularly if it was 100 yards or more away from what was left of the roadway. We sometimes made two or three trips up the road from advanced dumps and it was gruelling and dangerous work which resulted in an unusual number of casualties. Attempts were made to lay plank roads into the gun positions but the shelling was too intense to complete them, or if any progress was made, to maintain them. Another task took about ten of us and our teams to quarters in the partly-demolished Asylum at the western side of Ypres. From here we worked at a nearby railway switch unloading and hauling supplies through the city to forward dumps. This area was a favourite target for bombs and shells. In all we were quite busy and as far as I recollect we did not take time out during these weeks for bath parades.

A week after the last assault the Canadian Corps began to leave the area and on Tuesday, November 13th, we set out from our camp and travelled 12 miles to Caëstre. We remained here throughout the 14th and the latrine news was full of rumours that we were to return to the Salient with a vague connection to rumours of a new attack on another front. We continued our journey next day but rumours were rife of impending changes in our future movements throughout the remaining period beyond the opening of the Battle of Cambrai on the 20th until it ended on December 3rd after the successful German counter-attack. On that day, November 15th, we travelled 10 miles to Thiennes, east of Aire. On the 16th we made short progress to Ham-en-Artois through having to detour to cross La Lys Canal. On the 17th we made another short distance through Lillers to La Pugnoy and on the following day were back on familiar ground at Estrée Canche after twelve miles. On the 19th we moved forward to a camp near Mont-Saint-Éloi and were back again in the Vimy area between Arras and Lens.

WAR DIARY OF THE 4TH DIVISIONAL AMMUNITION COLUMN FOR OCTOBER 17, 1918:
Records show the unit to have been singularly fortunate in regard to Battle casualties. Only 5 having been killed and 38 wounded from April 1st to October 6th 1918.

There wasn't much excitement here except the rumours resulting from the Cambrai affair which started next day and notwithstanding such uncertainties, the granting of leave to Blighty was opened up This had been looked forward to by many during the eighteen months we had been at the front but I gave it scant thought because of the leave to Paris which I had opted for. Due to the heavy casualties in the Canadian Corps, including our unit, in 1917, the wheel revolved more speedily and I was told that I was nearing the point of eligibility for a 14-day leave. My name came up to depart on November 30th and with three or four others I left just after midnight on that date from a nearby railway station. We arrived at Boulogne at 7 A.M. and sailed at 2 P.M. arriving at Folkestone at four where we entrained and were in London at 7 P.M. With Bill Patterson and Odell I put up at the Maple Leaf Club and next day, December 1st, I sought out a tailor to have my new issue uniform and top coat adjusted to a reasonable fit.

On leave to Blighty

I made efforts to get in touch with my old associate in the bank at Chapleau, Bill Hogarth, who was now a sergeant in the Pay Office but we did not get together until Monday evening, December 3rd, when we had a pleasant meeting. We repeated this on Tuesday and that afternoon I had gone to the theatre to see *The Better 'Ole*. On Wednesday, December 5th, I finished arrangements to go to Scotland on the 11:30 P.M. train from Euston Station. I arrived in Glasgow at 8 A.M. on December 6th and spent two very uncomfortable days there in wet weather and kept to my satisfactory hotel room a good part of the time. The local press carried brief news of the Halifax explosion of December 6th. I had missed an enemy airplane raid on London on the 6th and was back in France before the next one came on December 18th. On Saturday, December 8th, I left by train at 9:30 A.M. for Edinburgh where the weather was better and I saw something of the city including the Castle. I was somewhat disillusioned next day to find that there were no pubs open on Sunday and it was my 24th birthday. I went to the Overseas Club in the afternoon for tea and while I was in the dining-room someone stole my overcoat so I had to stay there until another soldier of my size came in wearing a British-warm type of coat. The chances were long I knew but it paid off within an hour so with another coat, not quite so new, I took the 10 P.M. train back to London.

On the train I met Bobbie Anderson, a fiery Scot-Canadian, who I found had been released from Edinburgh Castle that morning after he had been confined for a couple of days because of some indiscretion and he was more bitter than usual against authority. I believe he became a minor labour union leader in Winnipeg in later years. I spent the remaining days of my leave with him and others of our unit whom I met up with and also with Bill Hogarth. At the Strand Corner House and the various service clubs such as the Maple Leaf Club and the Beaver Hut in the Strand one could usually find an acquaintance. The Duncannon Bar just off the Strand was a favourite haunt of Bill Hogarth's and he and I met there several evenings. On Monday evening, December 10th, he, Bobby Anderson and I saw the first act of *Bubbly* at the Comedy Theatre. In the bar during the intermission two officers of the New Zealand Medical Corps, a Colonel and a Lieut.-Colonel joined us and we had such an interesting session of drinking and conversation that we did not go back to the play. I received an invitation from the Nightingale family to visit them at their home in Chiswick so I went out there on Tuesday afternoon where I found that Mr. Nightingale had arrived unexpectedly from Paris. His charming daughter guided me through Kew Gardens and Richmond Park and after tea with the family I returned to the usual haunts.

In Canada the Military Service Bill had been enacted into law in August but the first call-up of conscripts was not made until October 13th when the Union Government had been formed. A general election was set for December 17th and polling of overseas soldiers commenced on December 1st. This involved a peculiar method under which we were not allowed to vote for a candidate by name but only by party affiliation. (This I believe was criticized by opponents to conscription but it seems to me to have been a sensible arrangement as it would have been a big chore to have had available throughout the British Isles, Europe and elsewhere a supply of ballots for every constituency at home). While in London I voted for a Union candidate in Winnipeg Center who turned out to be Major G. W. Andrews and he received the highest majority in the country. This was the first time I had voted in an election and was to be the last for 15 years as I did not take up residence in Canada after being discharged from the army until 1930.

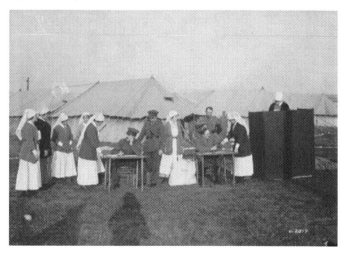

NURSING SISTERS AT A CANADIAN FIELD HOSPITAL VOTING IN THE FEDERAL ELECTION OF 1917

My 14 days' leave had well expired on December 15th when I left from Victoria Station at 7:30 A.M. for Folkestone. For some unknown reason we were detrained at Shorncliffe and marched from there to Folkestone. We sailed at 2 P.M. and after a touch of *mal-de-mer* arrived at Boulogne at 4 P.M. and spent a short night at a rest camp there. Our train left Boulogne at 5 A.M. and took us directly to Béthune where we arrived at 10:30 A.M. This was the next-to-last day for polling the soldier vote and during the journey I was surprised to see an officer making his way along the running board outside the car which was not of the newer inner-corridor type. He entered our compartment and solicited votes and when I told him that I had already voted he shrugged that off but I refused to submit—honest old soldier. At Béthune I was about as close to my unit as I could get but the Transportation Officer instructed me to take another train to Calonne Ricouart. It did not leave for several hours and I did not arrive at that destination until 5 P.M. Here I was informed that my unit was at Gouy Servins and not relishing the thought of remaining in the camp here overnight or trudging through the evening over the ten miles as I had done in September, I went up to the upper town where we had been stationed earlier in the year and obtained accommodation in my old billet but this time in greater comfort as I was paying a premium over the army compensation to such householders.

The next morning, December 17th, I reluctantly left my comfortable feather bed and after a leisurely breakfast of eggs and coffee in a convenient shop, I set off for the main road below, hoping to get a lift of some sort and was fortunate to catch a lorry which took me somewhat beyond the heavy hairpin grade at Gauchin. I arrived at Gouy Servins in time for the noon hour stables and put a hand to helping the men groom the animals of those who were still on leave. I found that our Colonel, notwithstanding the failure of the British to break through at Cambrai, was apparently of a mind that 1918 would be a year of open warfare. Events proved him to be right in his judgement but if it was formed as loosely as his methods of preparation it could have been nothing but a lucky guess. On this day I found that we were ordered to don gas masks just before putting the feed bags on the animals so that they would become accustomed to being handled by necessarily grotesque humans during gas conditions. To add to the simulated war scene a firing party of four men with rifles was stationed in the stable enclosure and ordered to discharge a few rounds while the rest of us struggled to put nose bags on the heads of mules, some of which showed by their complacent expressions that they thought that we were simple fools while others, not forgetting that they were veterans of the hell-fire of Passchendaele showed their disdain for mere rifles and gas masks by giving a merry hee-haw. Fortunately I had little of this tomfoolery as we prepared to move within a few days.

On December 21st we moved about three miles nearer to the front and took over good brick-floored and covered stables at Ablain-Saint-Nazaire. This village lies in the Souchez Valley, less than a mile behind the village of Souchez and the Arras-Béthune road. It had been almost completely destroyed as far back as 1915 when the ground hereabout was the scene of the great battle waged by the French in an effort to push the Germans beyond Vimy Ridge but left them still in command of the high ground after frightful losses on both sides and not redeemed until April of 1917. Above us to the north stood the Lorette spur which had been cleared of the enemy at that time but still held, as did all of the rolling ground to the south, remains of those who fought so dearly two years previously. A portion of the walls of the church was all that remained of the old village above ground. While our animals were well-provided with stables there was little provision for the men and everyone set to immediately to organize into groups which would forage for materials and build the numerous shacks in which we would live for the next three months. I joined five others, who between us, had prior rights to a large tarpaulin and before dark we had a comfortable wooden-walled home complete with wire netting beds and an oil drum stove. In this setting we prepared to celebrate our second Christmas at the front. Our canteen funds had prospered during the busy final months of the year and now in this very quiet spot the accumulated surplus was distributed in the form of a Christmas dinner. Turkeys and vegetables were purchased in the area behind us and at noon of the festive day we received one turkey and trimmings well-prepared to six men. One of our six was a confirmed vegetarian so the rest of us had bigger servings of our bird. Column H.Q. was adjacent to our lines and the Colonel and other officers joined with our officers in their celebration which must have been good as we found them about three o'clock in the afternoon tobogganing down the snow-covered slopes on pieces of curved elephant iron. Even nature was good that day, covering the battle-scarred earth with a light mantle of snow.

CHRISTMAS CARD SENT BY DRIVER HESLER TO HIS PARENTS BACK HOME, DECEMBER 1917

CHAPTER THREE

1918

It was a very quiet winter with very little activity on the front of the Canadian Corps from Hill 70 to opposite Vimy village, movements being limited to several interchanges of divisions. There were some working parties but with spring breaking early some of our farmer boys were put to ploughing the hillside behind our camp in preparation for the planting of potatoes and other army food crops. Who would harvest them? We played with the fantastic thought that we might remain here for the summer, almost reconciled to the belief that the war would go on forever, in ignorance of the great German thrust coming on both flanks in March and April to threaten the hold on the ridge ahead of us. Some of our work had been eliminated by extending the light railway system in the Lens and other Corps areas and operating them with motors instead of with mules as we did a year previous. We had frequent visits from officers of other units in the neighbourhood who brought their horses to be shod by our Farrier-Sergeant, Dave Hilland. He had learned his trade in Ireland and he was good at it. For these officers' mounts he did not use the ready-made army issue but fashioned the shoes out of buffer springs of 18-pounder guns which were worn out. A joke which passed at that time was that some speed-crazy officers were trying to get some lightning rods to be made into shoes for their horses by him. Dave came to a sudden end on his way to Bourlon Wood the following September.

We had received reinforcements after our losses at Passchendaele and my team had been allotted to another driver while I was on leave in December so for most of the remainder of the war I was somewhat of a driver emeritus and went on many excursions, usually on a horse, officially and unofficially, alone or in charge of a group of men, animals and wagons, from the forward area to well behind the lines, wearing no insignia of rank, but I was never challenged and never carried a pass except when on leave. Looking back on this in later years I was amused when I watched movies with war scenes to see the motions of challenge or to hear them when we progressed to talkies. Frequently on the pretext of exercising a horse I would ride over the old battlefield back to Château de la Haye or Carency or on foot explore the Lorette Ridge, Ablain-Saint-Nazaire or Souchez. Château de la Haye was that mysterious place around which was built the legend of immunity from German shells and bombs. One veteran has written that it was bombed in 1918 but the popular version among the Canadian troops which occupied the surrounding area from December 1916 to July 1918 was that the owner had some stronghold on the German authorities and had some guarantee against harm to his property and is recorded by Canon Scott, as of the end of 1917, as follows:-

> *"The Chateau was a large house of no distinction, and at the back of it was a pond whose clear waters reflected the tall, leafless trees which bordered it. One fact made the Chateau popular and that was, that, up to that time, no shell or bomb had fallen in the neighbourhood. It was said that the location of the Chateau was not to be found on the enemy's maps. Round about were huts with accommodation sufficient to house a whole brigade. The charm of the place was completed by our 4th Division having erected there a large and most artistic theatre, which would seat on benches nearly one thousand men. It had a good stage and a pit for the orchestra in front. This theatre, when our [1st Division?] concert party was in full swing, was a source of infinite delight to us all. It was built on the slope of a hill, the stage being at the lower end and a good view of the play therefore, could be had from all*

parts. The scenery was beautifully painted and the electric lights and foot-lights well arranged."

Nothing remained of Souchez except the large painted sign at the cross-roads – "This is Souchez" and rusty old iron that had once been a beet sugar factory. For weeks while we were here a working party of French soldiers was busy in the cemetery burying what could be found of their 1915 dead. A wooden cross was placed over each grave but in the grave there was seldom more than a small cotton bag containing God knows what. Later France erected a memorial structure at the end of the Lorette spur, not far from the Canadian Vimy Memorial.

The winter of 1917-1918 was a period of great campaign against waste. No more frying our breakfast bread in bacon fat; it was saved and turned in for a cash credit with which we bought cabbages and other supplies from the farmers. Signs were put up urging the soldiers to salvage under a sort of Boy Scout slogan "What have you salvaged today?" Those who used safety razors were cautioned against throwing used blades away. This may have applied only to our unit for I did hear that the Colonel had an idea that if these blades were planted with our potato crop they would be self-peeling. What metal we saved could scarcely compensate for that used in making private motor cars which were selling like hot-cakes in Canada at the time.

WAR DIARY OF THE 4TH DIVISIONAL AMMUNITION COLUMN FOR JANUARY 26, 1918:
Returns of men with knowledge of German called for.

The German Spring offensive

With the approach of Spring rumours became stronger of an impending German push. Our Colonel was placed in charge of preparations of reserve gun pits and interest in agriculture waned while working parties were sent out with picks and shovels to dig these pits. One fine Spring day the Colonel set out on a trip of inspection of this work with a party of officers, non-coms—and me. Why I was included I do not know except that it may have been as a horse-holder but as none of the officers ever got out of the saddle it was merely a sightseeing tour for me which nearly put me on the casualty list. The Colonel was a hard rider and he scaled Lorette Ridge in a style that would have put a Cossack to shame. Whenever he glimpsed a shovel, an iron bolt or an old paint brush he would shout "Salvage" and his groom would spryly gather it in. By the time we were descending the slope on the north side towards Hersin I was getting very keen about the game and racing my little western pony to keep up with the Colonel I failed to see a guy wire slanting to the ground from a telephone pole. Just in time I threw myself flat along my horse's back and managed to slip under the wire without falling off and saved myself from a broken neck. For the rest of the day I paid no attention to salvage.

News soon came to us of a great German thrust on a wide front to the south of us on March 21 with rumours of impending activities for us although for a few days following there was little indication of trouble on our immediate front. On that day the 4th Division was in the line north of Lens and on the 22nd-24th its lines were extended north to Hill 70 but by the 28th some of its battalions had been moved first in reserve near Mont-Saint-Éloi and went into the line that night so that by the 30th the entire Division was in the line in the Gavrelle-Oppy sector in front of Vimy Ridge. After midnight March 25-26 I was awakened in my bivouac by the Sergeant-Major and told "Doc, get up and take any horse you like, carry 48 hours' rations for man and beast and report to the Colonel at H.Q. as quickly as possible. I have ordered Tommy Mitchell to go with you as your horse-holder and I'll warn the piquet and the cook-house to prepare the rations for you".

WAR DIARY OF THE 4TH DIVISIONAL AMMUNITION COLUMN FOR MARCH 26, 1918:
At 2.am. orders received to 'stand to' & be prepared to move at 1.0 hours' notice.

I had never given much thought to winning medals but the mystery of the summons to one of the lowest rank may have stirred memories of historical heroic deeds. But prosaically, with men and beasts laden with bully beef and hard tack biscuits and bulging bags of oats and nets of hay, Tommy and I in this odd array covered the short distance to H.Q. and became part of a group of six of which the other four were N.C.O.'s from the other two sections, assembled before the Colonel who was perched on the steps of what had once been a house in Ablain-Saint-Nazaire. I gave him my name and rank and similarly identified my horse-holder which brought an angry remark that he had asked for N.C.O.'s and that while urgency required him to accept us he would later investigate this show of disobedience. He told us that he had learned that the enemy would soon be upon us and he wished to establish emergency measures of communication in the event of a break-through. He asked whether any of us knew where our Divisional Artillery H.Q. was located. It had been my firm policy since enlistment never to volunteer for anything but here in this "dramatic" moment I was caught within the silence of the others and broke down to declare that they were at Noeux les Mines (I had noted this a short time previously when passing through that town in travelling from Béthune on some mission). Accepting this, the Colonel majestically directed me "You will report with this message (handing me a sealed envelope) to the Staff Captain and be attached to H.Q. as liaison between it and me. You and your horse-holder will proceed there as quickly as possible without galloping your horses on the hard pavements". We set off immediately so I never knew what orders the others received. Down to Souchez and then parallel to the front line we followed the deserted Arras-Béthune road. An occasional flare over on the right was the only sign that men were mad at each other except for the devastation dimly discernible in the night. To break the monotony we broke the rules by galloping our horses for brief spells. Going through what was once the village of Aix (-Noulette) my mind went back to school days and "The Ride from Ghent to Aix" ("How they brought the good news from Ghent to Aix") by Robert Browning. The seven or eight miles were soon accomplished in Noeux les Mines, a town relatively free from destruction but now in complete darkness, leaving me uncertain as to where H.Q. were located. Finding a sentry we obtained directions and warnings that Head Quarters did not like to be disturbed at night. The house to which we were directed was in total darkness but a spot of light in the garden turned out to be a Signals station with a man on duty. He directed me to the proper door of the chalet with further warnings about wakening people at 4 A.M. Undaunted, I rapped loudly on the massive front door and soon was rewarded by a candle-light appearing on the stairway, held in the hands of a woman, and when she came to the door the light she carried revealed such a charming lady as to give another meaning to the warning not to disturb the military at night. Without hesitation she accepted my request that I be taken to the Staff Captain and led the way up the stairs to a junior officer who was aroused with some difficulty. Apparently impressed by my insistence that I must see the Staff Captain personally, but not without a further warning, we went together and roused the sleeping warrior. He read the message which I had presented and burst into such profanity that even I, a muleskinner, felt admiration: "Your . . . Colonel says we are going to retreat this morning. Who in hell told him what the Germans are going to do? You get the hell out of here and go back and tell your Colonel from me that he's a goddamned fool". Well, anyway the lady went to the door with me. We decided to return to our lines by coming round the mountain in a different direction so that we could have coffee and eggs in Hersin-Coupigny—somehow the emergency did not seem so serious now. This delayed us in getting to our lines until about eight o'clock and here we found the entire Column hitched in and packed up ready to march, apparently waiting for me to come back with the directions for our flight. I delivered my message, edited, to the Colonel who, quite plainly disappointed that we were not going to retreat, gruffly ordered that the parade be dismissed. Then Tommy and I had to retrieve our personal belongings and turn in our rations.

That our Colonel was not alone in his fears regarding the enemy is shown by the following from "*The History of The 16th Battalion (Canadian Scottish)*" (First Division):

> "On the night of March 25th/26th, it seemed as if the storm was about to break on the Canadians. The most positive report went about that the enemy was to attempt a break through from Hill 70 northwards. About one a.m., the 26th, the Battalion was ordered to get ready to move by five a.m. At five a.m. the Battalion 'stood to', but nothing happened, and at 8 A.M. Brigade ordered the 'stand down'." (page 252)

The 16th Battalion was then in divisional reserve position at "Fosse 10", a group of houses on the Arras-Béthune road at the foot of the Bouvigny Ridge. We had passed by here on our way north to Noeux des Mines and on our return we turned off the main road at this point to reach Hersin-Coupigny but all of this activity, if you can call it that, must have been indoors as we saw no signs of it.

While we were settling back into our quarters on the 26th the top brass of the British and the French were meeting at Doullens, not very far away and directly behind Arras, and naming Marshall Foch to co-ordinate the actions of the two forces. On March 27 General Currie issued a Special Order, probably composed by Col. Bovey: "The Canadians are soon to be engaged. . . . Under the orders of your devoted officers in the coming battle you will advance or fall where you stand facing the enemy." I do not recall that we were favoured with this message.

We hovered about for a couple of days and on the morning of Good Friday, March 29th, we finally did pull out of Ablain-Saint-Nazaire. Fritz was hammering hard at Arras and in the assault which had opened on the 28th had made some progress. We moved back to our old quarters at Gouy-Servins and sat there during a day of heavy rain and wild rumours. In the evening orders were given to hitch in and leave all kits behind. I was left in charge of what remained but could not get a word of information from the officers or N.C.O.'s as to what direction they were taking—I hoped it was eastward. Here I was a few miles from the front, if it was still where I had last seen it, with a G.S. wagon loaded with kit, two or three men on sick list, three ailing mules and not a complete set of harness available. Nothing to do but go to sleep and rest with only a hurried assurance that we would be picked up some time. We had only a small supply of rations so we and the mules ate sparingly at day-break and noon. Shortly after noon we were relieved to see one of our N.C.O.'s ride into camp with orders to join the unit near Arras. How we were to get there with the ill-assorted animals and heavy load was left to us to solve. With plenty of haywire and some rope we managed to get the three mules and the N.C.O.'s horse hitched to the G.S. wagon and away we went to provide some amusement along the road to the tired soldiers who were coming out of the line. Delayed by frequent stops for repairs, we were overtaken by rain, mud and darkness but we managed eventually to find our unit near Anzin. We slept that night in the deep galleries carved out of the chalk which honeycomb this part of the front. The next day, March

31st, we moved up to open horse lines at Madagascar Corner on the Arras-Béthune road near Arras and the excitement of the retreat was over but the shadow of Don Quijote still followed our Colonel. The line from opposite Arras to opposite Lens had been drawn back only slightly in the push which had started on March 21st but there was great intensiveness during all of these days. Liddell Hart says that Haig was "unskakingly convinced that the enemy's next attack would be a converging attack on the Vimy Ridge". The days were bright and clear and our observation balloons were up every day. There was a string of six one day stretching out between Arras and Lens overlooking the Douai plains when a fast single-seater German plane swooped down from nowhere and starting at the northern end of the line he wove under and over alternate balloons firing a hail of bullets at each one. At the southern end he turned and went back over his work to finish off any bags that were still aloft. It was all done so quickly that every bag was down before it could be pulled down or defensive measures taken other than bailing out by the observers and the German was away to his own lines untouched. It was an admirable piece of work but the burning balloons would have delighted only a pyromaniac on our side.

WAR DIARY OF THE 4TH DIVISIONAL AMMUNITION COLUMN FOR
APRIL 1, 1918:
During the day, the observation balloons near the camp were shelled by the enemy, and one horse on D.A.C. strength wounded by falling splinters. In the afternoon an enemy airman attacked the balloons mentioned, and brought down four.

Our days and nights were taken up with odd jobs, one of which caused some anxiety to our officers and sergeant-major. One morning I was sent off early to report in charge of three wagons to one of our batteries. Reporting at their horse lines I was told that we were required to salvage ammunition that had been left at various forward locations in shifting gun positions but that it could not be done earlier than at dusk. So we slept all afternoon, did our tasks and arrived back at our lines towards midnight to find the sergeant-major in a great fuss over our prolonged absence. His concern over the possibility that we might have been destroyed or captured by the enemy was touching. What virtues I held that outweighed selection of available N.C.O.'s for such jobs I'll never know.

The Canadian Corps was stretched out from below Arras to near Lens and there was great anxiety over its ability to withstand a concerted push across Vimy Ridge. Reinforcements were being gathered from all sources and additional defences were being hastily prepared against possible renewed assaults against the ridge. As part of these activities I was sent out at the head of a gang of men to clear a cross-country road and bury a telephone wire from the Nine Elms (which had disappeared from the scene east of the Arras-Lens road) to the Arras-Béthune road as an additional exit for our guns in case the line broke. Digging into the old trench systems for material to fill shell holes we uncovered what was left of British, French and German soldiers who had never had any burial other than that provided by hasty construction of trenches and who had lost all means of identification. Our road was never required for its intended purpose for it transpired that the push along the long line south of Lens had died out on April 5th. Amidst it all on Sunday, April 8th, we moved back a short distance to covered stables and hutments at Anzin-Saint-Aubin. The next day the Germans started their push from between Lens and Ypres, broke through the Portuguese and moved on towards Béthune and Hazebrouck. The Canadian Corps was not directly involved but we received General Currie's order that we must refrain from calling our gallant allies, the Portuguese "pork and beans". The threat of disaster waned and although there was a fresh attack on the Somme to the south of us and renewed assaults to the north, the real threat of a break-through had come to a standstill by the end of April. The Germans had, however, practically destroyed towns which we had known in earlier days, such as Béthune and Bailleul but we were cheered by the news of the heroic exploit at Zeebrugge and Ostend on April 22-23. Our duties remained unchanged and the main excitement that I recall was when a small party of our men, sent to Barlin for canteen and officers' mess supplies, filched some of the officers' whiskey, put their wagon into a ditch and suffered F.P. No. 1.

While we were here the Captain fell into a horse-trading mood and scouting around, found an Imperial unit that had some greys— our colour scheme in horses was as always, grey. With this deal my freelancing was over for a while and I was given a lead team of grey horses. One of the horses seemed familiar but I doubted that it could be old Bang that I had brought over from England two years earlier. Putting him to the sure test of mounting and touching his rump, identification was completed by the same old kicking and plunging that I had known until he faded in the severe winter of 1917 and was sent to base. I thought then that he would end up in a glue factory but here he was, still thin and somewhat greyer. A small world, even among horses.

On Saturday, May 4th, amidst wild rumours we were again on the move headed towards the rear along the broad tree-lined Arras-Saint-Pol road and camping that night in uncertainty at Vandelicourt, a journey of about 10 miles. On Sunday we were on the road again early, retracing our steps of yesterday with no inkling of what our final destination was to be. The day's trek ended at Acq where we took over stables and hutments. It was explained that we should have come here in the first place but an error had been made in orders. Looking back from following events however, it could be guessed that the Colonel had taken it upon himself to parade us up and down the road in view of German balloons to give a show of great activity.

For nearly three months we were to be out of gunshot (Big Bertha was trained on Paris) enjoying glorious summer weather and turning our minds to the possibility of a great Allied offensive with our Colonel again in his glory directing training for open warfare. During these days there passed through Acq Imperial troops which had been brought over from Palestine to bolster the scattered lines in France but as weeks went on without a call being made upon the Canadians to go into the line we felt that the pressing dangers were being overcome. The days passed in rifle drill, mounted drill, with and without wagons, parades and inspections. One fine afternoon the Colonel staged a great sham battle along the road that runs from Acq to Haut Avenes and the farm land lying on either side. We did not parade all of our wagons and animals but the drivers thus released, including myself, were armed with rifles and rode on the limbers. Thus arrayed and seated on the hot steel of wagons we were startled to see the Colonel mounted on his galloping horse rushing along our line firing his revolver into the air and shouting that the enemy was upon us. We riflemen were ordered to spread out through the fields to protect our line of wagons. After a period of aiming and snapping empty rifles some of us fell asleep in the convenient shooks of fodder that was being cut by the farmers while others chose to regard the farmers as the enemy and set them running at the ends of rifles. Not knowing whether we had been victorious or destroyed we were turned back to our camp where we prepared to move again.

On Wednesday, May 22nd, after a little more than two weeks at Acq, we moved farther back to La Comté, near the town of Houdain. Here we had open horse-lines and the men were billeted in barns with the usual manure pile in the court-yard formed by the angles of farmhouse and barn. The country hereabouts, undamaged by war except the incidentals of war, was very pleasant—rich fields on rolling hills, green trees and quiet roads. We had weeks of the same drill with added rifle practice at nearby ranges. I was excused from duty for over a week because of an affliction of boils and spent a peaceful time in the orchard behind our barn, reading and sleeping. This prevented me from attending the great gathering of the Canadian Corps for sports competition at Tincques, about 5 miles south, on July 1st. We entered some horses but I do not recall whether we won any prizes. From all accounts it was a great event attended by high military and political figures of Canada.

According to one of the many Spanish proverbs—"How beautiful it is to do nothing, and then to rest afterward"—but this comparatively idyllic life had to end sometime and on Saturday, July 13th, we left La Comté at 9 P.M. We made camp at Bray, near Mont-Saint-Éloi, at daybreak and remained there about two weeks while the 4th Division was in the Gavrelle-Oppy sector of the line. Near us were the horse-lines of an Indian battery, the men all wearing turbans and adhering to their native customs amidst the difficulties of active service. While we were here I was given the job of clerk for the quartermaster-sergeant and from then until the end of the war kept myself busy clothing the men and feeding them and the animals and keeping the unit equipped. At the time we were without a quartermaster-sergeant, the post being filled by a corporal pal of mine, Syd Bartlett, who was in my team when we left England. He and I took turns in making the regular visits to the Ordnance Corps depot for equipment and also to the ration dump where we were represented by Syd's brother. I soon became fairly proficient at dissecting quarters of beef and carcasses of lamb. All supplies received were weighed and the amount of poundage was divided by the number of officers, non-coms and men and distribution made to the three messes on this basis. Out of a quarter of beef about 3 or 4 pounds went to the officers' mess and it took a steady hand with a woodsman's axe and carpenter's saw to neatly separate this portion. It was much easier when we received frozen Australian rabbits as we did frequently that year. We carried several large chests loaded with replacement parts of 18-pounders and 4.5 howitzers and these had to be kept in good condition. From then until I left the Continent I was never on parade except to draw pay.

The Last Hundred Days

On Thursday, August 1st, we set off on another move, this time with a pervading spirit that something big was under way. We made camp at Aubigny, about 5 miles away, at midnight and remained there quietly all day. This was to be our final departure from the Vimy Ridge area but in later weeks we were to come back for temporary periods behind Arras. The next time I travelled along the Arras-Béthune road was in July 1938. I then visited the new Canadian Vimy Memorial on Bastile Day, July 14th, and on this holiday there were many French people thereabouts and at the new French Memorial at the end of the Lorette spur. Arras and Lens were rebuilt and although they were in the path of the fighting in 1940 and 1944 the movements were too rapid to permit any new serious damage in these cities and the Vimy Memorial which was "honoured" by a visit from Hitler in 1940.

On Friday, August 2nd, we left Aubigny about 8 P.M. Convinced that we were to have long night marches I packed our wagon so that our stock of clothing made a soft bed at the top of the pile and when tired of walking or riding on the box I would stretch out under the stars and have a little shut-eye. From Aubigny we headed south, through Avesnes-le-Compte and Humbercamps and made camp at Orville, near Doullens at daybreak. We had camped near here on our journey to and from the Somme in 1916 but now the weather was more favourable than in those muddy days. We had covered about 18 miles during the night. The next day we left Orville at 8 P.M. and covering another 18 miles made camp at Belloy-sur-Somme, seven or eight miles behind Amiens which was then almost a besieged city.

Setting out again at nightfall on Monday, August 4th, we crossed the River Somme and encircled Amiens so that by daybreak we were securely hidden in the woods in front of Boves, about 6 miles south-east of Amiens. The woods were full of troops and all were cautioned to keep under cover. Fires were not permitted and with a penetrating rain falling on the night of the 5th through the 6th it was very uncomfortable. I had my usual jobs to attend to and kept busy. During the night of the 7th our ammunition wagons started out to take up their positions for the expected break-through next morning. With the remaining wagons I left the woods about 4.30 in the morning of the 8th and halting on the high ground at the edge of the woods we saw the great outburst of firing that opened up this great battle. Remaining here until word came back for us to move up we occupied grand-stand seats for a great spectacle. Moving off, we progressed slowly, stopping for some time to lend a hand at a forward ammunition dump and eventually arrived at the point where our forward wagons had made camp in what had been no-mans land twelve hours earlier. Our line had advanced 8 miles during the day and progress was continuing. Everyone had taken on new life and the appearance of cavalry changed the scene of previous dull warfare.

On Friday, August 9th, while our section prepared to move on again I headed back over yesterday's road on horseback to bring rations to our dump gangs. The Roye road on which I travelled was the dividing line between the French and the Canadians and it was a busy track of mixed nationalities with soldiers of the two Allies and German prisoners. Returning in the afternoon I had some difficulty locating my unit but found them before dark at Maison Blanc, near Mézières. In my search I covered a lot of ground that had been in the enemy's hands the previous day and saw much of the guns and material that had been captured. This ground, straddling the River Luce, was broken and dotted with many small woods. It showed less the ravages of war than the ground we came upon next day.

> WAR DIARY OF THE 4TH DIVISIONAL AMMUNITION COLUMN FOR
> AUGUST 10, 1918:
> D.A.C. personnel 'dug in' as protection against enemy bombing.

We moved forward about five miles on Saturday, August 10th, and made camp near Beaufort which had been taken the day before. Ours and other horse-lines were spread out over a large expanse of bare plain behind the town and woods. We remained here two weeks, a period of very hot weather and rumours of all sorts. By the end of this time the line was settled for a while where it had been just before the Germans retired to the Hindenburg Line in the Spring of 1917. In the meantime, one day the Scots Greys halted near our lines and applied dye to their horses before going forward. Not long after a few of them returned and showed evidence of having encountered resistance. Another body of cavalry went through later and I did not see them come back. The minds of the "big" men were still tied to the belief that this service would be the means of winning the final battles and while they did some good and heroic work at this time they were not the proper instrument to break through fortified lines. We also saw squadrons of Whippet tanks going back and forth and they too had their short-comings, mostly mechanical. Enemy planes troubled us a lot here, bombing horse lines nearly every night. Bartlett and I had slept in a grave-like hole we had dug under our stores wagon which was good enough protection while the weather was dry. We took turns in going back to the Ordnance dump at a cross-roads in the rear area where my friend, W.O.1 Don Glendon, was in charge. Don always managed to have his stores dump as far behind the lines as possible and thus escaped damage. Ironically, in the dirty thirties he was a deputy sheriff at Niagara Falls and when he went to a farm to serve a dispossession notice he was shot at by the farmer. Camps of French soldiers were located near us and we had to keep a very close watch on our loose material. I was able to get rid of a lot of shag tobacco which the French accepted gladly after our men had found the issue too strong. To our right, from here forward, the French had taken over the line and their area included the town of Roye. In July 1938 I came through Roye from Paris towards Amiens and travelled along the nearby main road. Towns along the way had been reconstructed but I was particularly impressed by the unattractive new buildings in Roye.

The 4th Division sector was taken over by the French and the tour of the Canadian Corps in the Somme area was completed. On Saturday, August 24th, we abandoned this camp at 9 P.M. and moved towards the north. On the road towards Le Quesnel we fell in behind other units moving out and the line was spotted by German planes which bombed and machine gunned the moving stream of wagons. Our section escaped unhurt but severe damage was done to units ahead of us. We crossed the River Luce and camped at Aubertcourt at 1 A.M. on the 25th. A short but exciting trip. We remained here one day and on Monday, August 26th, left at 9 A.M. and travelled north about 15 miles across the River Somme to Toutencourt, a village west of Albert, arriving about four in the afternoon.

WAR DIARY OF THE 4TH DIVISIONAL AMMUNITION COLUMN FOR AUGUST 24, 1918:

Infantry crossing in front delayed movement. Enemy 'plane dropped bombs, apparently aimed at infantry. Two bombs fell near D.A.C. 3 men killed 10 wounded, 7 animals killed 5 wounded in No. 1 Section.

We left Toutencourt at 8 P.M. on the 27th and travelled about 10 miles farther north to Saint-Amand where we arrived at about midnight. We left here about noon on the 28th and moved another 10 miles north to Habarq, about five miles west of Arras, arriving at 5 P.M. and taking over stables and hutments. The Canadian Corps had moved north to take part in a new offensive towards Cambrai from the Arras area. This began on August 26th but the 4th Division was not engaged until the 31st. On Thursday, August 29th, we left Habarq at 1 A.M. Leaving this suburb on the south side of Arras at 5 P.M. we moved forward to Hénin-sur-Cojeul over ground that had been captured by the 2nd and 3rd Canadian Divisions in the push which started on August 26th. Bartlett had been replaced by a quartermaster-sergeant who left almost immediately for a "course" in something or other and most of the work was left to me. One evening while we were here I had to ride out on some duty and did not return until late. I now possessed a shining new white bell tent and while I was unsaddling my white horse near the tent a German bomber came over and scattered his load nearby. My white targets were no doubt too inviting and I was soon under a hail of machine-gun lead. No doubt this was the most "outstanding" horse since the Battle of the Boyne. Fortunately, the horse and I were on the edge of a deep shell-hole so quickly shoving him into it and crouching beside his bulk I passed a few nervous moments until Fritz gave up the rabbit hunt. Which reminds me that here we received for the first time Australian rabbits frozen in their skins, a change from beef and lamb, and stews of them, but sometimes a bit hairy when the cooks were careless in their skinning.

WAR DIARY OF THE 4TH DIVISIONAL AMMUNITION COLUMN FOR
SEPTEMBER 9, 1918:
Billets for personnel very good, now that tents and infantry shelters have been issued.

On Monday, September 2nd, our division started the push through the Hindenburg Line and we moved over a short distance to Chérisy where we remained for four days. On the 6th we left Chérisy in the evening and after travelling through ghostly Arras, camped at a western suburb, Duisans, shortly after midnight. On Sunday, the 6th we moved a few miles away to Gouves and remained here two weeks. The breaking of the Drocourt-Quéant line had been successful but the advance stopped short of the Canal du Nord and the Canadian Field Artillery had been drawn out of the line to rest and reorganize.

CANAL DU NORD, SEPTEMBER 1918
AN 18-POUNDER GUN IS HAULED THROUGH THE BREACH

On Sunday, September 22nd, we left Gouves at 3 A.M. and heading forward, camped at Croisilles at 9 A.M. in the area where preparations were under way for the crossing of Canal du Nord. While we were here I had a bit of a set-to with the Sergeant-major who accused me of adding salt to the bacon delivered to the sergeants' mess. We had heard of a lot of German atrocities but this was one on our side that I was sorry that I had not perpetrated, if I had had the time. I smoothed him over and he accepted my avowals of innocence, probably influenced by the fact that he had no one to take my place and he could not demote me because I was as low in rank as I could be. On Wednesday, September 25th, we moved a little way forward to Bullecourt, a name prominent in recent fighting, but completely devastated and only saved from comparison with the Somme in 1916 and Passchendaele in 1917 by the dry condition of the terrain.

War Diary of the 4th Divisional Ammunition Column for September 28, 1918:

Extending along the Eastern side, and about 150 yds from the Canal du Nord in this area, a row of tank traps was discovered. The traps consisted of Minenvefers about 6½ inch caliber placed upright in the ground with special fuzes replacing the ordinary Minenverfer fuze. Over the fuzes heavy 4 x 10 inch plank boards were placed, these in turn were covered with some loose earth to render them inconspicuous.

During the night of September 26th when the section moved forward to take up positions for the attack scheduled for early next morning, I was left on the edge of Quéant with four wagons for which we had no animals and several men who were "walking casualties". The Canal was quickly passed and our forces went on to Bourlon but our little party remained here for four days, most of which I spent on my horse exploring this desolated area which had been a vital point in the Hindenburg Line. One day while I was away from camp one of my charges, the Corporal Saddler, who had a twisted ankle, accompanied by one or two others, hobbled over to the nearby Casualty Clearing station to watch the loading of a hospital train which was already operating on the railway that had been re-established in a very short time after the ground was won. In the rush he was placed on the train and the next we heard from him he was in Blighty.

At last on September 30th the section could find time to send horses to bring us back to the fold and we set off through Quéant towards the Canal du Nord. This canal was in unfinished condition when the war began and held no water. Here it was built over low land by high banks which looked like the wall of China. My rescuers told me that they had lined up with their wagons in support of our guns directly behind the infantry that was to clear the canal and as soon as the way was cleared they had advanced through the captured breach in the walls into the open fields towards Bourlon. We had suffered a number of casualties. We rejoined the section at a point behind Bourlon Wood. Soon after I arrived I was summoned to the Captain's tent and I went with some forebodings but I knew that he could not demote me. I found that his section marking flag had been lost in the hurried movements and that no one had been able to find a replacement. Would I get busy and get one from Ordnance? Also, would I keep an eye on the German wagon which he had "captured" and see to it that his souvenirs were not lost? I checked the wagon which was full of oddments picked up along the way so far in the Canadian Corps' "Hundred Days" and found that he was even transporting a bath tub, a rather rare item in that part of France at the time. We remained here behind Bourlon Wood about a week. Nearby was a camp of West Indian troops who added to the noises of battle by their loud singing. They were employed principally as a labour battalion but considerably higher in standing than the numerous Chinese coolie gangs which had been imported for road building and other labour tasks behind the lines.

The 4th Division was being brought out of the line to rest and on Monday, October 7th, we left Bourlon Wood and went back to Chérisy where we arrived at 6 A.M. We were camped this time along the Sensée River and were here for a week in weather which had turned decidedly unpleasant in comparison with the time we were here a few weeks earlier. The Arras-Cambrai Battle ended on October 12th and since August the Canadian Corps had made advances of 23 miles. It was now moving northwards towards Douai.

On Sunday, October 13th, we left Chérisy and moved forward five or six miles to a camp behind a wood between Récourt and Lécluse in preparation for an attack on the Sensée Canal. We remained here nearly a week and had a few shells and bombs thrown at us. While here our supplies of winter underclothing and long leather boots were issued. When we left here on Sunday, October 20th we began to move more rapidly. We crossed the low lands of the Sensée River at Lécluse and then went on to the Sensée Canal which had been crossed by the 4th Division infantry on the 18th. This was my first crossing on a pontoon bridge and while I had some trouble with my horse I was amused by the antics of the mules when they felt the bridge bobbing under their feet. Circling on to the Douai-Cambrai Road to Aubigny-au-Bac where we camped on the banks of the Sensée and its marshy lands I was busy immediately with getting in rations and returned to camp to find that I would have to go back to our previous lines and pick up men and equipment left behind. We had occasional casualties among our animals and with the Captain's souvenir wagon requiring at least two mules or horses we were now always a little short on draught. In this instance my trip was postponed until morning when I set off with a couple of wagons to retrace our journey of yesterday. Although I was determined that I would not traverse the great half-circle of the previous day I found that the bridges had not been replaced where I thought they should be and so scouting the area as Marlborough did here in 1711 I finally resigned myself to the longer but more secure journey.

WAR DIARY OF THE 4TH DIVISIONAL AMMUNITION COLUMN FOR SEPTEMBER 30, 1918:
From commencement of CAMBRAI operations 21-9-18 to date inclusive, dumps operated by this unit have issued approximately 192,573 rounds Field Artillery Ammunition.

I had been told that I was to catch up with the section at Mastaing, about 10 miles farther advanced and there I rejoined it on the 21st after a journey on which every mile showed increased occupation by French civilians. Mastaing was fully populated by excited people relieved of German domination for the first time in four years. Our unit had received a great welcome when they arrived here earlier in the day. On Tuesday, October 22nd, we moved a few miles to Escaudain, behind the larger town of Denain which had been captured a few days before. The next day we moved a few more miles to Oisy, a village behind Valenciennes. It had been captured on the 21st. We had a bad time during the latter part of the week we remained here. Our horselines were shelled heavily on several occasions with the consequent loss of a number of animals. The villagers were torn between resentment at our making them a target and gratitude for the horse and mule flesh which they were able to salvage after each shelling. On each occasion, as soon as the immediate danger had passed they would rush out of the village to our lines and hack away at the carcasses and fight for the choicest bits. I am sure that a nice piece of mule steak was a great treat to them. One evening at dusk I was issuing rum to some of the men who had been up to the guns when Fritz sent over a couple of shells which overshot the horse lines and came close to my tent which I had not dyed. The three or four of us standing within the tent flattened ourselves on the ground. One of the men, trying to make himself as small as possible was crowding his head into my stomach forcing my behind against the hot oil-drum stove which I had stoked up to take off the evening chill. The smell of singeing cloth convinced us that we had been hit but when the shelling ceased we found that there was no damage except a neat hole about two feet in diameter in the tent where my head had been a few minutes earlier. It was no consolation to us that it was discovered next day that we were camped on the wrong side of the village in plain view of the enemy's observers! I made a few trips to Denain and found it to be a very quiet and almost undamaged place. It was still quite close to the front and most of the inhabitants were staying indoors. On the outskirts there was a large German cemetery that had suffered from some shelling. One inhuman spectacle was the straying lunatics who had been let loose from confinement in hospital by the Germans when they retired from the city. It was reported also that they released all inmates of hospitals who suffered from venereal disease.

WAR DIARY OF THE 4TH DIVISIONAL AMMUNITION COLUMN FOR OCTOBER 23, 1918:
Many civilians in the village, who were left without food of any description. The majority have not eaten bread for two weeks.

On Friday, November 1st, while our division was taking the city of Valenciennes, we moved across the rear to Thiant, south-west of Valenciennes. Sunday the 3rd, we moved north-east to Le Poirier on the northern outskirts of Valenciennes where our quartermaster-sergeant joined us and I suffered from severe toothache. We were quartered here in the steel plant which stood on a ridge between two villages.

Harold Hesler

> ### WAR DIARY OF THE 4TH DIVISIONAL AMMUNITION COLUMN FOR NOVEMBER 7, 1918:
>
> Many civilians entering the town [Valenciennes] from neighbouring villages, bearing their goods & chattels on all manner of improvised vehicles. The city was formally handed over to civil authorities by military authorities at 1100 hours today. The ceremony being held in the Place d'Armes, and amongst those present being H.R.H. The Prince of Wales, Lt-Gen. Currie the Canadian Corps Commandant and numerous other Canadian officers. Infantry and artillery of all units who took part in the occupation were present, the 4th Cdn. Division being predominant.

LA CARTE DU THEATRE DE LA GUERRE

MAP OF THE EASTERN AND WESTERN FRONTS FROM A GERMAN PROPAGANDA BOOKLET "LIBERATED" BY DRIVER HESLER AT VALENCIENNES, NOVEMBER 3, 1918

On Tuesday, November 5th, we moved into the city of Valenciennes and the QMS and I took over a house facing the Champ de Manoeuvres while our section was quartered around that square. Our address was 13 Rue des Glacis. The house had been perforated by shells in several places and apart from this there were signs that it had been ransacked but it was still in pretty good shape. Making a bed of several upholstered chairs I lived there until next day when I went over to a street near the station where I had been directed to find an Army dentist who extracted a wisdom tooth. Great damage had been done to the railway station which the Germans had blown up before they left, but in general the city was fairly intact. The 4th Division was withdrawn from the line on November 7th for a rest period which overlapped the armistice.

Early in the morning of Monday, November 11th when I went to the orderly office to check up on the nominal roll for my indents I was told, hush, hush, that a message had been received at Column H.Q. stating that the war would end at eleven o'clock that morning. Strangely, it created no emotional effect and the same applied to most of the men who were paraded at eleven o'clock to receive the announcement and also orders to give the animals an extra good grooming. The end of the war had been expected to occur before winter set in but I think most of us hoped that it would end on German soil. I announced that there would be an extra rum issue that evening but practically all chose to attend the cinema. In the last three months they had received lots of rum but never an opportunity of seeing a motion picture. One or two joined me in a quiet drinking party at my billet and we discussed the future.

WAR DIARY OF THE 4TH DIVISIONAL AMMUNITION COLUMN FOR NOVEMBER 11, 1918:
Armistice came into effect at 1100 hours today, the news being very quietly received.

On Saturday, November 16th, we started on what we thought would be a long trek to Germany but the 4th Division never got there. Out along the Valenciennes-Mons road there was a steady stream of civilians returning to their homes pushing barrows, pulling carts and carrying babies, wholly concerned with making progress as rapidly as possible. A crossroad had been blown up and temporarily repaired by our Engineers; and the railway running along the road had also been blown up and rails were hanging in the air in many places and at one point a long stretch of rails and ties was neatly wrapped over the roof of a building. We crossed the border into Belgium "without customs inspection" that afternoon and pulled off of the main road into the town of Elouges where we remained for four days. I was billeted in the clean white-washed home of a working man whose hospitality was already strained by several refugee relatives. Nevertheless, Dixon, the Q.M.S., and I were forced by them to accept the main bedroom as our own. Four days amid the brick kilns of this town and on Wednesday, November 20th, we were off again, headed towards Mons. The Engineers had done rapid work in repairing the damage left by the Germans but refugees were still coming through. We took up quarters at Cuesmes, a coal-mining suburb of Mons. I was billeted in a very clean house on the main street occupied by an old coal-miner, his wife and their son who had been conscripted by the Germans for labour behind the lines and recently returned. Food was still scarce amongst these people and they partook of only one meal after a very light breakfast. That consisted usually of vegetables that were put on the stove about noon and left to cook until the evening when it was a thick mass that had some chance of sticking to their ribs. Over this tiresome meal and later when neighbours might drop in the gossip flew fast and sometimes bitterly. On our first day in the town one of our new neighbours, a woman accused of having lived with the German officers, was taken from her house and in the street was shorn of her hair—a very temporary scarlet letter. During my three weeks here I made several visits to Mons on duty and I was greatly impressed by the broad avenues and huge trees of this city now so famous in British history. There were long lines of men and women waiting to be interrogated as suspected collaborators.

> War Diary of the 4th Divisional Ammunition Column for November 16, 1918:
> The first stage in the move forward to complete the occupation of the German Rhinelands was made today when the column took the road for ELOUGES at 10:00 hours.

In Cuesmes we again enjoyed the luxury of steaming baths at the mine wash house where the miners hang their street clothes away up among the rafters at the end of a rope running over a pulley, the lower end being locked with a key carried by the owner of the clothes. When he is in the mine this raiment hangs on high and when he has finished for the day and bathed they are replaced by his soggy work clothes left to dry for the morrow in the heat of the bath house. Speculation was rife as to our future. Were we going to be demobilized here, move to Germany or return to England? Considerable unrest developed to die out with news of a move towards the east and by despatching men on leave to Blighty. Amid all this I quietly passed my 25th birthday.

Back to Blighty

On Thursday, December 12th, after helping the Q.M.S. pack for an early move I left Cuesmes and headed towards the opposite direction on leave accompanied by Johnny Gibson. Walking a few miles to Jemappe on the main road we were fortunate to get a lift on a Royal Flying Corps light truck and were in Valenciennes in fast time at noon. We had to remain at a rest camp here until next morning and then we missed the train to Calais, it being Friday the 13th. We left at 9 A.M. for Boulogne expecting to be in London that evening but transportation was in a bit of a muddle and we did not reach Boulogne until 4:30 A.M. on Saturday the 14th. At 6 A.M. we were placed on a train and taken to Calais where we remained from 8 A.M. until 1 P.M. when we boarded ship and arrived at Dover at 4.30 P.M. A train brought us to London by 8 P.M. and I went to the Maple Leaf Club. During our stop-over in Calais I met up with an old acquaintance from Welland who was on his way to England to take examinations for a commission. A little late in the game but there was still uncertainty as to how many Canadian troops would be assigned to the occupation of Germany and for how long.

My activities in London centered around the Strand Corner House and the Duncannon bar with some sightseeing and theatres thrown in. I had at least one meal at the Maple Leaf Club and that was served to me by Princess Patricia and Miss Martha Allan of Montreal. I found that some of my mates who were also on leave had gone to Ireland so I decided to go there too. The regimental paymaster had given me a cheque for £20 when I left on leave and now I paid a visit to the Pay Office on Millbank and with the assistance of Bill Hogarth raised another £9 which was probably more than I was entitled to as my pay-book shows that I did not draw any further pay until the following February 8th.

I left Euston Station at 5 P.M. on December 18th and travelled by train to northern England where I crossed by steamer to Belfast, arriving at 7 A.M. I put up at a hotel, the Prince of Wales I think, and soon found some of my friends from the section. We had a pleasant sober several days—visited Harland & Wolfe shipyards, saw a soccer game played by girls, went to church and after a dull Christmas Day left on the morning of the 26th by train, arriving in Dublin at 1 P.M. Several of us toured the city in the afternoon but our uniforms attracted such hostile glances that we took refuge in a cinema until it was time to leave for the port of Kingstown and there we found that the ship would not sail until daylight. We slept on the docks and went on board to sail at 9 A.M. We crossed to Holyhead and from there travelled by train through beautiful Wales to arrive in London at 7:30 P.M.

By this time I should have been on my way back to Belgium but I still had a little money left and having heard that Johnny Gibson who had come over with me had been picked up by the Military Police and was on his way back to Canada I thought that I would try my luck. The M.P.'s did not even glance at me but with an expired pass I could not obtain sleeping accommodation in any of the usual places and I spent my nights in rooming houses in Victoria Street that were not operated strictly nor attractively.

About December 30th President Wilson was in London on his way to the opening of the Peace Conference and he was given a rousing reception as his carriage went along The Strand. Following in another coach and four were the Prince of Wales and Lloyd George, the latter looking like the cat that had swallowed the canary. Seeing that the world was in such good hands I decided to return to Belgium and I left from Victoria Station at 7:30 A.M. on December 31st, comfortably settled in a first class compartment where the military guard had placed me in return for a half-crown.

I need not have been in any hurry. We made the trip to Dover and Calais in good time but on New Years Day 1919 we were moved from

Calais to Boulogne and remained there for two days and then it took three days on a train to reach Mons, via Abbéville, Amiens, Arras, Douai and Valenciennes. I left the troop train at Mons and travelled on secondary trains to a point south of Brussels where, later in the evening of January 6th, 1919, I rejoined my unit at a small village, Bierges, a few miles south of Wavre, all in the general area of the Battle of Waterloo of 1815 and to become an important point along the River Dyle in May 1940.

CHAPTER FOUR

1919

In Bierges I again took over the duties of quartermaster-sergeant without rank and had as my assistant my old friend John Zoller. We occupied a house on the main road, a small part of which had been allocated to the Y.M.C.A. for a canteen. On January 16th and 17th I had 48 hours leave in Brussels and was accompanied by Rod Macdonald. The capital city had not suffered from shelling or bombing during the war and while the citizens were somewhat more pleasant to foreigners than those in some other parts of Belgium it was a rather gloomy city in the dull winter days.

During this period I was never on parade except to draw pay. It had been decided that no additional Canadian troops would go to Germany and in the shuffle it was decided that the Corps would return to Canada in numerical order of divisions - 1st, 2nd, 3rd and 4th - so that we would be amongst the last to leave. Our wagons and heavy equipment and all animals except a few saddle horses were gradually dispersed so that there was little for the men to do but sit around and grouse or walk to Wavre for a watery glass of beer. On some of these early Spring mornings "my groom" would bring "my horse" to the house and I would go for a ride in the forests and hills of this area. I was probably the only private in the British forces that had a horse and groom. During this period there came to our H.Q. as Adjutant, a Captain T. H. Atkinson, who had gone overseas in a battery with the First Contingent. Through the scuttlebutt it was learned that he had been with the Royal Bank before enlisting and probably no one except himself expected that one day he would be General Manager of the bank.

WAR DIARY OF THE 4TH DIVISIONAL AMMUNITION COLUMN FOR MARCH 22, 1919:
30 Riding, 36 L.D. horses and 50 mules turned over to Belgian Government.

The Ordnance Corps had set up an establishment a few miles away in a small chateau at Limelctte where they were taking in all of the equipment of the 4th Division under the direction of my old friend, W.O.1 Don Glendon. Early in March he asked me to join his group to compile and maintain records of this equipment so, in agreement with the Quartermaster-Sergeant who had returned to duty, I went off and took up residence in the chateau which was almost bare of furnishings except for army cots. Apart from a number of men who handled the articles as they came in there were about six of us who functioned as the "executive", all of them sergeants except of course Glendon and me. At Don's request I typed out an order and at the first opportunity had a visiting officer sign it, raising me to the rank of sergeant. This was tacked to the office door and taking stripes from the ample stores under my control to sew on my sleeves I became for the first and last time an N.C.O. but without pay for the rank. My old friend, Sid Bartlett, was one of the group and somehow had been raised from corporal to sergeant since I had last seen him.

ORDNANCE UNIT, LIMELETTE, BELGIUM, 1919

We had a rather pleasant life here with light duties which permitted visits to the *estaminet* outside the gates and allowed time for me to listen in on the party line telephone connecting all units of the division and keep myself informed of what was going on in higher circles. We had commandeered a mule and cart and one fine day the Armourer-Sergeant and I set out with this equipment to visit the infantry battalions to check up on matters relating to rifles of the division. This took us throughout the area of the Battle of Waterloo. We were well entertained by each battalion and a good time was had by all, so much so, as I note from my pay-book, that at 12th Infantry Brigade H.Q. I was able to touch the paymaster for 80 francs, equal to two months pay allowance, on April 17th. This was probably as a precaution against financial isolation as the Division was already on the move towards England while we remained behind without access to a pay-master and having to find out our own supply of food and finally the means of transportation to the coast.

By the end of April the last of the 4th Division, except our little "executive" group had left for England. I recall listening in on a telephone conversation between Atkinson and the Staff Captain in which the latter asked whether the Column was ready to move out. Atkinson said that everything was in order except that there was one man missing—a man named Hesler and they did not know where he was. They might have asked the Q.M.S. of our section and I was still receiving my mail through it, but apparently nobody cared. Anyway, the Staff Captain did not as he decided the matter quickly with "Let the s.o.b. stay here and rot—be ready to move on (date)". He could not have remembered that I was the man who had roused him early in the morning a year before at Noeux-les-Mines.

I had compiled thick ledgers and in them had a complete record of every item in the establishment of a division. Medical supplies and costly instruments, such as range-finders, watches, etc. had been in my custody and these were delivered to some central authority. Shortages in such items had to be covered by a sworn statement of the commanding officer of each unit that they had been destroyed in action. We did not accept any such declaration unless accompanied by a jug of rum and, in the case of the 11th Brigade, two jugs, as Brig. Odlum had never allowed his men to have a regular rum issue and I had seen a large supply under the cot of his Q.M.S. when I visited it on my tour with the Armourer-sergeant. We got rid of our surplus rum somehow and when I asked the D.A.D.O.S. what I should do with my records he directed me to throw them on top of a pile of harness and leave them there! All of the horses and mules of the Canadian Corps had been sold to the Belgian Government at £40 each (too high a price I would say) and all of the stores and equipment such as we had gathered together was turned over to the British Government to be paid for at an appraisal price. I often wondered how the Belgians trained these animals to their method of driving one or a team with only one line.

On May 6th Glendon, Bartlett and I were, I believe, the last of the 4th Division left on the Continent and on that evening we set off together from Ottignies station to find our way back to England. We spent the night in Namur as there was no train through to the coast until next morning. We boarded that at 6 A.M. but were chucked off of it at Charleroi. We could not get much assistance there except that we might be able to get on the mail train from the Rhine which went through in the evening. We were at the station at the appointed hour and during the short stop of the train we made a deal with an N.C.O. for some francs to allow us to ride in a mail car. There, hidden behind mail sacks, we arrived at Boulogne at 7 A.M. on Thursday, May 8th, and sneaking out of the terminal were able to make arrangements to board a cross-channel ship at 10 A.M. From there we had no trouble and arrived in London from Folkestone at 3:30 P.M. Being nearly broke I rushed down to the Pay Office where with the help of Hogarth I was able to draw £1 so I squandered some of it on a room at the Shaftesbury Hotel instead of going to a military hostel.

The next morning I took the train to Bramshott Camp where I was attached to No. 1 Section, 4th Canadian Divisional Ammunition Column, Group 21, B Wing, which was to be demobilized in Montreal, the point which I had selected. I was received with much courtesy as a sergeant and on Saturday, May 10th, I was rushed through all formalities, including a declaration that I had not suffered any physical impairment during my period of service, and was given a pass to take me to Aberdeen with a friendly warning that my leave might be shortened by changes in sailing plans. I drew £8 pay which was about all that was coming to me as accruals to the end of May left me with a balance of only $18.30. This was an accumulation of only half my pay as I had, upon going overseas, assigned the other half to my father who held this available to me in Canada for small personal expenses there and I had also drawn on it to meet disbursements on other leaves.

I arrived in London on the afternoon of Saturday, May 10th, and before I could get around to making arrangements to visit Scotland I received a telegram ordering me to return to Bramshott to prepare for sailing to Canada. I said good-bye to Hogarth, not expecting to see him again until maybe sometime in Canada but we did not sail as early as the telegram to me might have indicated. Riots broke out in the Canadian Military camp at Rhyl in Wales and we were delayed while a large number from there were hastily brought into the group which was to sail in our ship along with added service personnel including Hogarth. I loafed around Bramshott until Sunday, May 18th, when we were marched to Liphook station where we entrained for Southampton and at noon embarked on the Aquitania, then one of the largest ships in the world. A strike was in effect in the harbour and we did not leave the dock until noon on Monday the 19th. There were no tugs in service and the big ship was brought out into open water under her own power. It was an interesting display of seamanship. With the added passengers the ship had over 7,000 on board and the poor privates had to sleep in shifts with a large part of them in hammocks.

RMS AQUITANIA, STILL IN HER ANTI-SUBMARINE CAMOUFLAGE IN 1919

Befitting my rank I occupied a cabin with several other sergeants instead of taking turns with those of lower rank in occupying hammocks. As nobody seemed to know who I belonged to I received no orders for duty during the voyage as other sergeants did. I met up with several old friends on board, including Hogarth who had been rushed out of his post at the Pay Office in London to do similar work on board ship where I received a cheque for $100.63 made up of:-

Balance on discharge to Canada	$18.30
Pay and allowance to June 2, 1919	2.20
Civilian Clothing Allowance	35.00
1st Payment, War Service Grant	70.00
	125.50
Less -	
Assigned Pay - June	$15.00
Boat expense money	4.87
Train expense money	5.00
Cheque	100.63

Although exchange values began to fall after the Armistice so that at this time the values of francs and pounds sterling were below par in terms of Canadian dollars we were still charged at par in this final settlement. Another twist was that having been paid only $2.20 for service in the month of June 1919 the army book-keepers deducted $15 for assigned pay for that month.

We arrived at Halifax on a rainy Sunday afternoon, May 25th, and entrained immediately on the Intercolonial, arriving in Montreal early on May 27th. Sir Robert Borden, the then Prime Minister of Canada, has different timing as recorded in his Memoirs, page 966:

> "On May 18th, I boarded the Aquitania at Southampton at 6.15 p.m. My diary for that day concludes as follows: 'I should be very happy to return to Canada were it not for politics'. We sailed the next afternoon May 19th. My niece, Kate MacLatchy, was among the passengers. The voyage was without incident of note and I spent much time studying the Treaty. We reached Halifax on May 25th, where I was met by my wife and several of my colleagues. We left Halifax for Ottawa early that morning."

My brother Norman, then living in Montreal, met me at Bonaventure Station from where he marched with us up Peel Street to Montreal High School where the Mount Royal Hotel now stands. This was my first sight of the center of the metropolis. Our group lolled around until early afternoon when I turned in my kit and received my discharge as "Acting Sergeant" as also shown on my final pay-book issued on board ship. However, when I later received my Service and Victory medals I found that they were inscribed on their edges to Gunner H. G. Hesler although I had always previously been listed as "Driver".

After a couple of days in Montreal, where I gathered together some civilian clothes, I set off, still in uniform, for Humberstone where my father and mother who had not seen me since early 1915 welcomed me at the tiny Grand Trunk station with the hope expressed that I would remain with them for some time. Within a few weeks I was away again, this time to Cuba, and that is another story.

During those weeks I found that the wearing apparel which I had sent home from Winnipeg early in 1916 still fitted me. While I was at home John Zoller visited me for a few days and I made the short trip to Saint Catharines to visit George Wilson. During a visit to Toronto I was surprised to meet several of my western comrades and Nobby Clark was already on the police force of the Queen City. Just the other day I met with Bombardier Alder, now a Q.C. in Brandon, who was on his way to Europe and I read in the sports pages that Ching Johnson was still interested in hockey. During the 1930's I met with Ching several times when he came to Montreal as a star on the New York Rangers team.

THE END

APPENDICES

Ostend
Bruges

Dover
Folkestone

Dunkirk

BELGIUM

Calais

PASSCHENDAELE

Poperinge

YPRES

Steenvoorde

Courtrai

Boulogne

Hazebrouck

Lys R.

Lille

Neuve Chapelle

Tournai

Festubert

Béthune

Noeux-les-Mines

Ablain-St-Nazaire

LENS

Scarpe R.

Acq

VIMY

Douai

Valenciennes

Mont-St-Eloi

FRANCE

Arras

Denain

CANAL DU NORD

CAMBRAI

Bapaume

Courcelette

Albert

SOMME

Somme R.

Dieppe

AMIENS

St-Quentin

La Fère

Rouen

Beauvais

Soissons

Aisne R.

Oise R.

10   5   0   10   20   30   40   50

Seine R.

MILES

Evreux

Paris

Marne R.

MAP OF NORTHEASTERN FRANCE AND BELGIAN FLANDERS
PRINCIPAL ENGAGEMENTS OF THE CANADIAN EXPEDITIONARY FORCE 1915-1918

Extracts from Harold Hesler's travel diary in 1938

[Editor's note: the events of July 1 and 2, 1938 are included to show that, ironically, Harold Hesler's second ocean voyage to Europe was more eventful than the first, notwithstanding the absence this time of German submarines.]

Friday, July 1st. In a drizzling rain embarked on *S.S. Ascania* of Cunard Line at eleven in the morning . . . Sailed at noon . . .Weather somewhat clearer in the afternoon as we passed Three Rivers but raining when we stopped in the stream at Quebec at 9:30 A.M. to take on passengers and disembark a few honeymoon couples making the short trip from Montreal. The illuminate Falls of Montmorency were faintly discernable through the mist as we came towards the Isle of Orleans.

Saturday, July 2nd.   Awakened by a sharp jolt and lurch which I thought was caused by a heavy wave but looking out the port-hole I saw only the peaceful waters of the Saint Lawrence and returned to bed. At eight o'clock we were wakened by our steward presenting the Captain's compliments and would we get dressed and go on deck as quickly as possible. . . . . it became quite obvious that the ship had been badly damaged as a result of hitting a rock early in the morning when we felt the shock. Our baggage was hastily packed and transferred to the *Beaverford* by the Government tender *Citadelle* which had come alongside. . . . Some delay was occasioned when the tender was required to assist the *Ascania* to run further aground . . . We were advised that we would be given the choice of transferring to the C.P.R. ship *Montclair* at Quebec on Sunday and going direct to England or of sailing from New York on the *Queen Mary* on July 6th.

THE VIMY MEMORIAL

Thursday, July 14th.   Crossing the wide Oise River over a new bridge replacing the one blown up by the British in August 1914 we took the road towards Montdidier and traveled over rolling country with fields of growing grain.   After traveling about ten miles we came upon the first signs that we were entering that part of France which had been fought over for four years in the last war. There were still some traces of trenches and revived villages rebuilt in rather ugly style. Bearing right we came to the town of Roye, a name familiar to us in August 1918 when we were advancing away from Amiens with Roye on our right. The town had been part of the battle line for the greater part of the war and had been completely destroyed.   It is now rebuilt, the most outstanding building being the new church of modernistic design. We stopped for a moment and entered the church to find the severe lines of its interior in great contrast with the many old buildings we had seen. Turning left onto the Amiens road we soon came to the country I had known in August 1918 but what a difference now! The dips and rises in the road but both sides crops were growing abundantly and the old deserted and partly destroyed villages of Beaufort and Beaucourt were now restored and surrounded by woods. Domart and the marshy valley of the Luce River where I camped on August 8th, 1918 seemed familiar although rebuilt and Hangard Wood has grown again. Most impressive was the short distances between points which I used to think were far apart when I rode my horse up and down this road. We were soon approaching Amiens and could discern Boves Wood on our left where the Canadians had so successfully hidden out for several days to spring their surprise attack on August 8th, 1918. Entering Amiens we went directly to the Hotel Univers where we had an indifferent lunch. Noticed a loaded bus arriving marked "London to Tyrol Lakes" loaded with Britishers and a number of other Britishers who were obviously visiting the old battle ground. After lunch we visited the Cathedral and spent some time there admiring the architecture and stained glass. Left the city by a wide boulevard connecting with the road to Albert over the Somme plains. Stopped at Albert for a few minutes to grasp how much had been done to rebuild a large town that had been a rubble heap when I was here in 1916. Then the spire of the church still stood with the figure of the Virgin and Child tumbled over at right angles looking down on us as we sloshed through the muddy street below. Later even this was laid flat. Now the church and surrounding buildings have been reproduced in ugly new red brick and it seemed to me that I liked it better as it was in 1916. Once again I was going up the Bapaume Road but now in incomparable comfort. Over to the left towards the River Ancre where we had our horse lines in a sea of mud there were now fields of green crops and beyond, against the horizon stood the British National Memorial with its 73,000 names of missing men. Where the road forks at La Boiselle the huge craters are still to be seen slightly diminished in size by nature in twenty-two years but still so large that they will probably remain long after some of the erected memorials have been razed in new wars. Near Pozières we stopped and entered a British cemetery—a real memorial—well maintained. The Butte de Warlencourt still stands but is now a green grass covered mound standing in peaceful fields. The road to Arras branches off the Amiens-Cambrai on which we were traveling before it reaches Bapaume so we did not visit this rebuilt town which always seemed to be a rainbow's end in 1916. All of this part had been pretty demolished in the war and while it had been rebuilt mostly of permanent material, much use of our old corrugated and elephant iron was still being made. Due to repairs in progress on this main road we were forced to detour over narrow roads winding back and forth over the railroad line and I recollected that I had come this way over this railroad on a slow return from leave in January 1919 when all about was in ruins, except the railroad line which had been pushed on in a semi-repaired condition as the enemy retreated. Entered Arras at a point near the railroad station with its large open square. With its reconstructed buildings the square and other parts of the city formed a much different picture from the one formed years ago on horseback excursions through Arras. Arras has been a centre of more or less importance for fifteen hundred years but to Canadians it has an interest that overshadows the earlier vicissitudes of the city with its warriors, cave, tunnels, tapestry makers and Robespierre. On through the Grande Place where not a soul was to be seen and then into the Petite Place, equally deserted. We seemed to be the only sightseers on this holiday. Both squares are enclosed by houses rebuilt or in process of being rebuilt in the Flemish style in which they originated five hundred years ago. At one end of the Petite Place is the Hôtel de Ville and its lofty belfry which provided a fine target for the Germans who put 69 shells into it one day in October 1914. These buildings have been reconstructed in their old form. Temporarily lost in the winding narrow streets we finally found our way out to the northern suburb of Sainte-Catherine where I once lived in a cellar retreat while working with the trench mortars in 1916 at Écurie and Roclincourt, small villages lying on either side of the Arras-Lens road on which we were now traveling. Turning off to the left we came to the Canadian National Memorial on Vimy Ridge overlooking the plains of Douai stretching out below us to the east but now the view gained by the battle of April 1917 was obscured by mist. I had seen many pictures of this memorial published when Edward VIII unveiled it in 1936 and the disapproval formed then was unchanged by this visit. My disapproval may be expressed in the words of another: "Admitting the greatness of the event which the monument is there to perpetuate, the latter seems unnecessarily huge, and the thought is impressed upon one: how needless to attempt to equal an achievement by means of a memorial comparable in size?" I am sure that the Canadians who lie in the many beautiful cemeteries along this line believe that they are the true memorial and that the huge pile of granite costing millions is ostentatious. We visited the trenches in this piece of Canada and found them somewhat lacking in attention although this may have been due to the many French people who were swarming over the place on this national holiday. Now, in peacetime, the value of possession of this ridge is seen in the possible extended view to the east from the Memorial and to the west from these trenches. Mont-Saint-Éloi monastery ruins still stand on the ridge to the west and below us runs the valley of the Sanchez River where we spent many days. Dipping down through Angres we crossed the Arras-Béthune Road and climbed to the tip of Lorette Ridge where the French have erected a huge memorial to commemorate the great battle of 1915 in which they lost many men but gave the enemy the first nudge off of the higher ground. From the lookout provided we could see below us Ablain-Saint-Nazaire with the ruins of its church, and other villages still fresh in my memory for we spent most of 1917 and the early part of 1918 in this area. The afternoon now far advanced we moved on down into the valley again and passed through the village of Souchez which used to have a sign "This was Souchez" but is now a collection of homes of coal miners the same as Lieven and other suburbs of Lens, the centre of many coal mines. All of these places were completely destroyed and rebuilt but look drab in this late light. Turned towards Lille we sped over good roads on level ground with slag heaps all about us marking the coal mines. Carvin and Seclin were the only towns of any size along the road from Lens to Lille. Lille was an important supply point for the German Army until the last few months of the war during which time all of this area behind Lens was in their possession. Although within range of the Allies' guns, Lille was never shelled by them but as we entered through the rather shabby suburbs there was still evidence of the destruction caused by the Germans in 1914 and the explosion of the munitions depot in 1916.

. . .

Friday, July 15th Left Lille about 10 A.M. after driving around the principal streets and viewing some of the interesting buildings. . . A few miles beyond Armentières we came to the Belgian border and with little delay were passed through the customs gates, but at that we tarried long enough to have many urchins swarm over us with the old war-cry: "Gimme penny mister". After leaving the border town of Le Bezet we could see the range of low peaks beginning on the west with Mont des Cats, standing over my point of first arrival in 1916, Godewaersvelde, Mont Noir, Mont Rouge, Mont Kemmel and Messines Ridge. Over the ridge and through Wytschaete past Shrapnel Corner and so into Ypres. How quiet it seemed in the streets leading to the square with little activity other than housewives scrubbing their housefronts and sidewalks. In the main square the peaceful scene of souvenir stalls, the half-rebuilt Cloth Hall and the spire of the new Cathedral conflicted with the awakened memories of the ruin and danger of the many days and nights I rode a mule across this target. Regretting lack of time to visit the old Asylum, Vlamertinghe and Poperinghe, we passed out of the city through the new Menin Gate erected as a British Memorial. Once again on the Zonnebeke road which used to be a narrow trail through seas of mud and now is a cobbled road between fields of splendid crops and rows of houses. The railroad whose embankments once gave us a sense of security now runs in good order over the road twice as it curves through Zonnebeke and rises slightly into Passchendaele over the ridge of sorrowful fame. Along this road we see many direction posts pointing to many British cemeteries and here and there piles of steel shell splinters which had been cleared away from the lands now in crops. At Westroosbeke we came over a somewhat better road and left behind us the area which had been churned by shell and bomb but from time to time as we traveled in a northerly direction we saw a number of pillboxes that had been built by the Germans and were now used as root-cellars or cow shelters. Onward over the low-lying lands to the old city of Bruges where we arrived at noon to find most of the shops closed or about to close for the noon hour but we were able to make a few interesting purchases.

. . . .

Saturday, July 16th. . . . Left Brussels about three o'clock and were soon driving through a large forest of huge trees. In Wavre after 20 years nothing seemed familiar but at Bierges a couple of miles farther I recognized my old billet from where I used to set out in February 1919 to ride around this part of the area where Wellington and Napoleon had skirmishes prior to the battle of Waterloo which was fought a few miles from here. We decided not to visit the battlefield which I had seen several times. At Limelette we stopped to take a picture of the chateau in which I lived in March and April 1919. Continued on over rough cobbles through Ottignies, Genappe to Nivelles and then through a coal mining district where we were held up for as short time by a miner's funeral. We were now in the area where the British first made contact with the Germans in 1914 and soon were in Mons driving through the wide boulevard with its huge trees and stopping in the Grand Place where we had tea in a sidewalk café overlooking the square.

Harold Hesler

TRIPLICATE

3rd. DIV. AMN. COL. **ATTESTATION PAPER.**

No. 311972
Folio.

CANADIAN OVER-SEAS EXPEDITIONARY FORCE.

QUESTIONS TO BE PUT BEFORE ATTESTATION.
(ANSWERS.)

1. What is your surname? ... Hesler
1a. What are your Christian names? ... Harold Gustave
1b. What is your present address? ... Suite. 1. Bettes Block, Winnipeg. Man
2. In what Town, Township or Parish, and in what Country were you born? ... Humberstone, Ontario.
3. What is the name of your next-of-kin? ... (Father) Hesler, Gustave
4. What is the address of your next-of-kin? ... Humberstone. Ont.
4a. What is the relationship of your next-of-kin? ... Father.
5. What is the date of your birth? ... Dec. 9th. 1893
6. What is your Trade or Calling? ... Bank Clerk.
7. Are you married? ... No.
8. Are you willing to be vaccinated or re-vaccinated and inoculated? ... Yes
9. Do you now belong to the Active Militia? ... No.
10. Have you ever served in any Military Force? If so, state particulars of former Service. ... No.
11. Do you understand the nature and terms of your engagement? ... Yes.
12. Are you willing to be attested to serve in the Canadian Over-Seas Expeditionary Force? ... Yes

DECLARATION TO BE MADE BY MAN ON ATTESTATION.

I, Harold Gustave Hesler, do solemnly declare that the above are answers made by me to the above questions, and that they are true, and that I am willing to fulfil the engagements by me now made, and I hereby engage and agree to serve in the Canadian Over-Seas Expeditionary Force, and to be attached to any arm of the service therein, for the term of one year, or during the war now existing between Great Britain and Germany should that war last longer than one year, and for six months after the termination of that war provided His Majesty should so long require my services, or until legally discharged.

(Signature of Recruit)

Date January 20th. 1916 (Signature of Witness)

OATH TO BE TAKEN BY MAN ON ATTESTATION.

I, Harold Gustave Hesler, do make Oath, that I will be faithful and bear true Allegiance to His Majesty King George the Fifth, His Heirs and Successors, and that I will as in duty bound honestly and faithfully defend His Majesty, His Heirs and Successors, in Person, Crown and Dignity, against all enemies, and will observe and obey all orders of His Majesty, His Heirs and Successors, and of all the Generals and Officers set over me. So help me God.

(Signature of Recruit)

Date January 20th. 1916 (Signature of Witness)

CERTIFICATE OF MAGISTRATE.

The Recruit above-named was cautioned by me that if he made any false answer to any of the above questions he would be liable to be punished as provided in the Army Act.
The above questions were then read to the Recruit in my presence.
I have taken care that he understands each question, and that his answer to each question has been duly entered as replied to, and the said Recruit has made and signed the declaration and taken the oath

before me, at Winnipeg this 20th day of January 1916

(Signature of Justice)

ENLISTMENT FORM SIGNED BY HAROLD HESLER, JANUARY 20, 1916

94

Description of ____Harold Gustave Hasler.____ on Enlistment.

Apparent Age 22 years 1 months.
(To be determined according to the instructions given in the Regulations for Army Medical Services.)

Distinctive marks, and marks indicating congenital peculiarities or previous disease.
(Should the Medical Officer be of opinion that the recruit has served before, he will, unless the man acknowledges to any previous service, attach a slip to that effect, for the information of the Approving Officer.)

Height ____ 5 ft 8½ ins.

Chest measurement { Girth when fully expanded ____ 34½ ins.
Range of expansion ____ 2 ins.

Complexion ____ Clear

Eyes ____ Bluish Grey

Hair ____ Dark Brown.

Scar from Operation

appendicitis 1913.

Religious denominations.

Church of England
Presbyterian
Methodist
Baptist or Congregationalist
Roman Catholic
Jewish
Other denominations. ____ Lutheran.
(Denomination to be stated.)

CERTIFICATE OF MEDICAL EXAMINATION.

I have examined the above-named Recruit and find that he does not present any of the causes of rejection specified in the Regulations for Army Medical Services.

He can see at the required distance with either eye ; his heart and lungs are healthy ; he has the free use of his joints and limbs, and he declares that he is not subject to fits of any description.

I consider him* ____ fit ____ for the Canadian Over-Seas Expeditionary Force.

Date ____ Jan. 14th, ____ 1916

Place ____ Winnipeg. Man ____

Medical Officer.

*Insert here "fit" or "unfit"

NOTE.—Should the Medical Officer consider the Recruit unfit, he will fill in the foregoing Certificate only in the case of those who have been attested, and will briefly state below the cause of unfitness :—

CERTIFICATE OF OFFICER COMMANDING UNIT.

____ Harold Gustave Hasler ____ having been finally approved and inspected by me this day, and his Name, Age, Date of Attestation, and every prescribed particular having been recorded, I certify that I am satisfied with the correctness of this Attestation.

(Signature of Officer)

Date ____ January 20th ____ 1916

Commanding No. 3 Section, Divisional Ammunition Column

BACK OF ENLISTMENT FORM

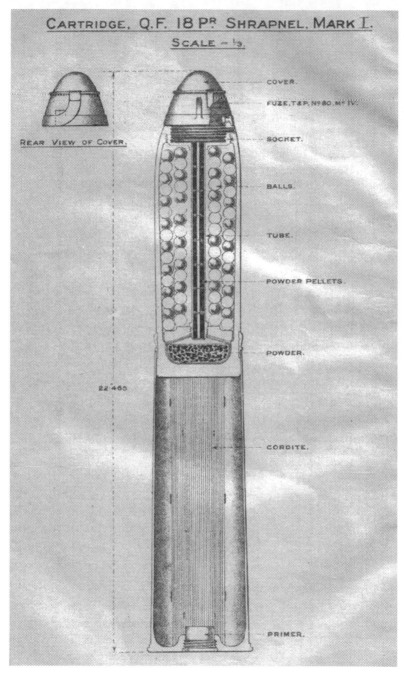

*TECHNICAL DRAWING OF AN 18-POUNDER SHRAPNEL SHELL
FROM THE FIELD MANUAL CARRIED BY DRIVER HESLER
FOR THE DURATION OF THE WAR*

FIELD ARTILLERY TRAINING
1914

---

1. Object and method of training

1. The object of training is to fit all ranks for the performance of their duties in war.

3. As soon as a man enters the service, every endeavour should be made to foster in him a soldierly spirit.

. . . The privileges which he inherits as a citizen of a great empire should be explained to him, and he should be taught to appreciate the honour which is his, as a soldier, of serving his King and country.

94. Training young mules.

1. Young mules are naturally timid and easily startled, but they are, as a rule, docile and easily broken in, if treated with great kindness and patience. Rough treatment of any kind must be avoided as likely to prove fatal to the successful training of the mule.

230. Casualties on the move.

2. . . . if a firing battery mule becomes a casualty, its load will at once be transferred to the relief mule, another relief mule to replace this one being immediately ordered up from the first line mules.

231. Casualties in action.

2. Ammunition wagons may be ignited on being struck either by projectiles or bullets, the liability increasing with the amount of wood used in the construction of the wagons or boxes. Should a wagon be ignited by a projectile there is usually very little danger of it blowing up immediately; attempts should therefore at once be made to put out the fire, remove the ammunition from the wagon, or move the wagon away.

236. Divisional ammunition columns.

1. Each divisional ammunition column consists of four sections, of which the first three carry small arm and 18-pr. ammunition and the fourth ammunition for the howitzer and heavy battery.

EXCERPTS FROM THE POCKET MANUAL CARRIED BY DRIVER HESLER

PAGES FROM DRIVER HESLER'S PAY BOOK
SHOWING A TOTAL OF $1.10 PER DAY FOR MEN IN THE FIELD

"SHOULD AULD ACQUAINTANCE BE FORGOT . . ."

Editor's note: This photo of Harold Hesler and a mule was taken during an excursion in the hills near Jundiai, not far from Sao Paulo, Brazil, in March 1932. Hesler was then the General Inspector of the Royal Bank of Canada, and was on a tour of inspection of the Bank's branches in South America. Beside the photo he had written "Should auld acquaintance be forgot".

Fifth row: Meloche, Ogmundson †, Alder, N/A
Fourth row: Whitlock, Macdonald, N/A, N/A, N/A
Third row: Hesler, Wilson, G.H. †, Westberg, Ramsay
Second row: Parsons (son), Ellis, Hogg, Foster, Bartlett
Front row: Parsons (Sr.) †, Moseley, N/A, N/A, Wilson, F., Cpl. Williams

FIFTH ROW: *N/A, N/A, N/A, N/A, N/A*
FOURTH ROW: *HORN, ZOLLER, KEEL, JOHNSON, BECKETT*
THIRD ROW: *JUDGE, HARVEY, N/A, BEALES*
SECOND ROW: *CRABB, N/A, LUCE, N/A*
FRONT ROW: *SGT. MCFADDEN, LT. MILES, SGT. PRESTON*

Fifth row: N/A, Lewis, Slidders, Horton
Fourth row: Beckett, N/A, N/A, Foote
Third row: Parkinson, Williamson, Brown
Second row: N/A, Legge, Stone, Verrinder, N/A
Front row: N/A, Owens, N/A, Baldwin †

MEN OF THE 3RD SECTION, 3RD D.A.C., C.F.A.
(LATER, 2ND SECTION, 4TH D.A.C., C.F.A)

[Editor's note: This list was drawn up mainly on the basis of one which E.D. Alder had drawn up for a reunion of the Section in the early 1950s. Alder, who was then a Queen's Counsel practicing law in Brandon, Manitoba, sent it to Harold Hesler in 1963. Where there are discrepancies with the list of names which appeared in the *Manitoba Free Press* on March 7, 1917 (see page 6), the latter was given precedence. The entries for those killed are based on the First World War Book of Remembrance.]

(see page 6)

* indicates original enlistment   †indicates killed

* Adams, R.B.
  Aikens, (Sgt. Maj.)
* Aikenhead, J.B.
* Alder, E.D.
* Anderson, R.G.
* Armin, L.
* Armstrong, E.D.
  Arnott, T.
* Atkinson, R.B.

  Bailey
* Baldwin, H. †
* Bannister, A.D.
* Bartlett, A.
* Bartlett, S.J.
* Beales, L.B.
* Beales, G.H.
* Beckett, A.E.
* Beckett, A.G.
* Beecham, Alex
  (Cpl)
* Berry, Pete
* Bonner, Frank

  Booth
* Bowman, A.E.
  Brady, A.
* Brown, C.H.
* Brown, W.J.
* Brownell, J.E.
  Bruton
* Bullock, W.B.
* Burr, E.J.
  Butchers, Sgt.
  Butchers, R.
  Butler

* Campbell, H.
* Campbell, W.J.
* Capel, Robert (Bdr)
  Carr (QMS)
  Carpenter
  Chabot, L.
  Chamberlain
* Chisholm, A.
  Church, T.
* Clark, W.

  Clarke, (Bdr)
  Clendenning
* Clifford, W.C.
* Clift, Fred
  Code, E.V.
  Cole
* Coleman, J. (Cpl)
  Coleman, W.
* Coller, R.A.
  Collins, I.J. †
  Cook (Capt.)
  Coppen (Lieut)
* Cotter, A.
* Crabb, J.
  Cummings (Lieut)
* Currie, J.

  Dalziel
  Dand, E.B.
* Davey, G.
* Davies, W.H.
* Davis, A.
* Davidson, J.

Dawson (Sgt)
* De Ath, G.H.
Dixon (QMS)
* Dixon, W.A.
* Dollimore, B.
Donahue
* Dunbar, J.M.

* Edgecombe (Lieut)
* Ellis, S.M.
* Evans, G.

* Farquharson, W.
* Farthing, W.H.
* Foote, H.
* Ford, H.S.
* Fort, H.
* Foster, C.
* Fowler, H.
Fowler
Frobisher

Gagnon
Gannon, J.S.
Garrett
* Gartside, F.
Gault
* Gaunt, A.W.
Gibbons
Gibbs
* Gibson, John
* Gillies, A.
Glazier
* Gooderich, A.A.
Green

* Hague, E.W.
* Hainsworth
Harrison, S.M.

* Harvey, W.H.
* Hean, F.
Hendy (Capt)
* Hesler, H.G.
Hewitt
* Hewitson, J.
* Hicks, H.
* Hilland, D.A. (S/ Sgt)†
* Hoggarth, M.E.
* Hogg, S.A.
* Horn, A.K.
* Horton, C.
* Horton, J.
Horton
* Houston, C.
Hughes, James †

Jardine
Joel
* Johnson, I.W.
* Judge, F.W.L. (Bdr.)

* Kay, O.T.
* Keel, W.J. (Bdr)
* Kirby, J. (Bdr)
* King, J.H
* King S.J..
Kirkby, W.
* Knowles, (Cpl)
* Krueger (Capt)

* Lawrence
* Lees (Bdr)
* Legge, G.L.
* Lewis, E.J.
Little, D.
Little
Lloyd, Harry

* Loyd, Tommy
* Low, T.
* Luce, W.G.

* Macdonald, A.
* MacDonald, Rod
* Macdougal
* MacFarlane, J.A.
* MacGibbon, S.
* Mackey, R.
Malloy
* Manson, F.
* Marshall, C.R.
Mason (Vet. Sgt.)
* Maughan, C.
Mayhew
* McFadden (Sgt. Maj.)
* McKay (Bdr.)
* McKibben (Cpl)
* McPhail, J.
McTaggart
* Meek, W.
* Meloche, D.M.
* Middleton, A.A.
* Miles (Lieut)
* Mitchell, J.A.
* Milford, W.
* Miller, J.R.
Modeland, C.
* Modeland, E.W.
Moore
* Morley, F.R.
* Mosley, W.
* Mowatt, W.
Murphy
Murray
* Murray, P.

* Noble, W.J.

* Ogmundson, H. †
  Orange, F.
  Othey
* Owens, A.E.

* Parker, S.O.
* Parkins, A.
* Parkinson, W.
* Parsons, Fred C.
* Parsons, R.C. †
* Patterson, J.
* Patterson, W.
* Perry, Sam
* Phelps, Sidney †
  Phillips (Bdr)
  Phippen (Lieut)
* Pockock, R.E.
* Preston, (Sgt)
* Pryce, H.
* Price, S.
* Price W.G.

* Quinn (Sgt)

* Ramsay, G. S.
  Rankin
* Rathwell
* Redfern, R.P.A.
* Reid, D.
  Roberts
* Rombaugh, W.
  Rothwell (Bdr)

  Savage, Frank †
* Sawkins, F.F.
* Scott, D.C.
* Scott, J.G.A.

  Shaw (Capt)
* Sherlock, E.V. (Lt)
  Sherriff
* Shields, W.
  Shortt, S.
* Simpson, W.B.
* Sinclair
* Slidders, A.
* Slidders, D.
* Smith, W.S.
  Speak
  Spratt
* Squires, W.B.
* Stevens, L.
* Stone, C.E.
* Strange, G.T.
  Studely

* Tees, Percy
* Thompson, J.A.
  Thompson
  Tiernan
  Townsend
* Trew, T.
  Turner (Sgt. Maj.)

* Vaughan, A.F.
* Vaughan, D.T.
* Vaughan, F.
* Verinder, B.
* Verinder, F.H.
* Vincent, W.E.

* Wade, R.
* Walker, G.
* Walker, W.
* Wallace, R.
* Wallace, P.F.
* Wallace, W.T.

* Wantuk, L.
  Ward
  Webb
* Welch, R.
  West (Cpl)
* Westberg, H.
* Wheeldon, L.
* Wheeler, W.
* Whitlock, A.L.
* Whitlock, J.G.
* Whitlock, L.S.
* Wilkinson, E.J. †
* Wilkinson, J. H.
* Wilkinson, J.
* Wilkinson, M.
* Wilkinson
* Williams (Cpl)
* Williamson, J.K.
  Wilson, G. (Sgt)
* Wilson, Fred
* Wilson, G.H. †
* Wilson, H.
* Wrathall, G.J.
* Wright, A.J.W.

  Young (Capt)

* Zoller, J.L.

LEXICON

18-pounder: the standard British quick-firing field artillery piece used throughout the First World War and into the Second.

Bdr.: Bombardier, or artillery corporal.

Blighty: slang for "Britain".

C.F.A.: Canadian Field Artillery.

D.A.D.O.S.: Deputy Assistant Director of Ordnance Services, the senior supply officer in a Division.

Farrier-Sergeant: an N.C.O. with specialized skills in the shoeing and care of horse's hooves.

F.P. No. 1: Field Punishment Number One, which consisted of being tied to a wagon wheel or post for up to two hours a day, for several days. It replaced flogging in the British forces in 1881.

G.S. wagon: General Service wagon.

Horse line: outdoor, unsheltered stable area.

Limber: a two-wheeled cart used to support the tail of a field gun when hauled, and to carry ammunition.

N.C.O.: non-commissioned officer (corporal, sergeant, staff sergeant).

Q.M.S.: Quartermaster Sergeant, an N.C.O. responsible for a unit's stores and supplies.

W.O.1: Warrant Officer First Class, the rank held by a Regimental Sergeant-Major, the highest non-commissioned rank, and often considered higher in authority (if not rank) than most junior commissioned officers.

In 1916, a young bank clerk from the Niagara region joined the Canadian Artillery and was shipped off to France and Belgium. Three and a half years later, he returned to Canada and rejoined the bank, eventually to become one of its most senior officers. This is his own account of that interval, during which he survived the battles of the Somme, Lens, Vimy Ridge, Passchendaele, and the Canadian spearhead of the Allied advance during the last one hundred days of the war.

About the Author

Harold Hesler was born near Port Colborne, Ontario in 1893. At the age of 16, he was hired by the Royal Bank of Canada as a junior clerk at its branch in Welland, Ontario. In January, 1916 he resigned from his position as accountant at the branch in Winnipeg, Manitoba, and enlisted in the Canadian Artillery as an ammunition driver. He saw action in all the major engagements of the Canadian Expeditionary Force in France and Belgium from October 1916 until the end of the First World War. Following his return to Canada in May 1919, he rejoined the bank and remained there until his retirement. By that time, the Royal Bank of Canada had become one of the largest banks in the world, with Hesler serving in various executive positions including General Inspector, Secretary of the Bank, and head of its extensive foreign operations. He died at Montreal in 1982, survived by his wife Edith Aimée Gravel, his son William Hesler, and two grandsons.

William Hesler is the author of *"Muleskinner: the European War of a Niagara Artilleryman"*, published in 2010. He lives in Montreal.

U.S. $13.95

ISBN 978-1-4620-0352-5

90000

9 781462 003525

iUniverse®
www.iuniverse.com